Feminist Marxism or Marxist Feminism:
a debate

Network Foundation For Educational Publishing

Network Foundation is a voluntary membership foundation. General policy and overall objectives are established by the membership and administered by an elected Executive Committee. An Advisory Board, appointed by the Executive from the ranks of the membership, advises on all publishing decisions.

Foundation Objectives:

1. To facilitate the development of a healthy and responsible Canadian-controlled post-secondary book publishing sector.

2. To assist in the production, dissemination and popularizing of innovative texts and other educational materials for people at all levels of learning.

3. To develop more varied sources for critical works in the Humanities and Social Sciences.

4. To expand the readership for Canadian academic works beyond a select body of scholars.

5. To encourage the academic community to create books on Canadian topics for the community at large.

6. To develop works that will contribute to public information and debate on issues of historical and contemporary concern, thereby improving standards of education and public participation.

The Network Basics Series, one of the Foundation's activities, provides inexpensive books on the leading edge of research and debate to students and the general public.

This Network Basic is published by Garamond Press. Please direct all enquiries to 163 Neville Park Boulevard, Toronto, Ontario M4E 3P7.

Feminist Marxism or Marxist Feminism: a debate

Pat Armstrong

Hugh Armstrong

Patricia Connelly

Angela Miles

Introduction by
Meg Luxton

Garamond Press
Toronto, Ontario

A NETWORK BASICS BOOK

Copyright © 1985 by Garamond Press
Acknowledgements
Studies in Political Economy: A Socialist Review for:

Armstrong, Pat and Hugh Armstrong, *Beyond Sexless Class and Classless Sex: Toward Feminist Marxism*. No. 10, Winter 1983.

Miles, Angela, *Economism and Feminism: Hidden in the Household. A comment on the Domestic Labour Debate*. No. 11, Summer 1983.

Connelly, Patricia, *On Marxism and Feminism*. No. 12, Fall 1983.

Armstrong, Pat and Hugh Armstrong, *More on Marxism and Feminism. A Response to Patricia Connelly*. No. 15, Fall 1984.

Reprinted with permission

All rights reserved. No part of this book may be reproduced or transmitted in any form by any means without permission in writing from the publisher, except by a reviewer, who may quote brief passages in a review.

Garamond Press
163 Neville Park Boulevard
Toronto, Ontario M4E 3P7

Canadian Cataloguing in Publication Data

Main entry under title:
Feminist Marxism or Marxist feminism: a debate

(Network basics series)
Articles reprinted from: Studies in political
economy, v. 10-12, 15.
ISBN 0-920059-12-0

1. Women and socialism – Addresses, essays, lectures.
2. Feminism – Addresses, essays, lectures.
I. Luxton, Margaret. II. Studies in political
economy.

HX546.F45 1985   335.4'088042   C85-098653-2

Cover Design: Walter Augustowitsch
Printed and Bound in Canada

A grant from the Canadian Studies Program of the Secretary of State assisted in the development of the Network Basic Series

Contents

Meg Luxton	Introduction	vii
Pat Armstrong/ Hugh Armstrong	Beyond Sexless Class and Classless Sex: Towards Feminist Marxism.	1
Angela Miles	Economism and Feminism: Hidden in the Household. A Comment on the Domestic Labour Debate.	39
Patricia Connelly	On Marxism and Feminism.	53
Pat Armstrong/ Hugh Armstrong	More on Marxism and Feminism. A Response to Patricia Connelly.	63

Contributors

Hugh Armstrong teaches Humanities and Sociology at Vanier College, Montreal.

Pat Armstrong teaches Sociology and Women's Studies at Vanier College, Montreal.

Patricia Connelly teaches Sociology at St. Mary's University, Halifax.

Meg Luxton teaches Women Studies at Atkinson College, York University, Toronto.

Angela Miles teaches Sociology at St. Francis Xavier University, Halifax.

Meg Luxton

Introduction

In the early days of the women's liberation movement, heady with their new-found understandings of oppression and liberation, feminists set out to explore the terrain of male domination and female subordination. They took with them what maps were available and as they travelled, they confirmed, redrew and charted anew. Of the existing theoretical maps, marxism was the among the most promising. It had a well-developed theory of class oppression, it acknowledged women's oppression and argued that a radical social transformation was necessary for women's liberation. One of the major debates which has engaged feminist theoretists is the extent to which marxism in fact provides a useful guide. Some feminists reject marxism altogether but most contemporary feminist theory has been profoundly influenced by it. The relevance of the marxist tradition for feminist theory has been widely discussed and its central concepts and methods scrutinized in the feminist literature. Feminists have criticized marxist theory for largely ignoring women, for sex-blindness, and for failing to theorize gender. While some claim that marxist theory is basically sufficient as is as long as sex/gender is added on, others maintain that feminism profoundly challenges the basic premises of marxism and argue that it must be reworked, its central categories and assumptions reconceptualized in light of feminist analyses of gender relations.

Feminist theory recognizes that women's oppression is rooted in women's location in the family. Marxist feminists used the analytical tools of classical marxism to show that what women do in the home is in fact socially necessary work which contributes to the maintenance and reproduction of capitalist society. This understanding sparked what became known as "the domestic labour debate". Multidimensional and highly contentious, this debate nevertheless generated a range of conceptual breakthroughs which both sharpened feminist analyses of the family-based roots of women's oppression and introduced gender analyses into marxist theory.

The articles in this collection present readers with an overview of several key debates in feminist theory, especially on domestic labour, and shows the consequences of different analytical pespectives.

The articles all address the relationship between feminism and marxism, asking to what extent marxism in general, and the domestic labour debate in particular, help us understand the oppression of women in capitalist society. All four writers share a committment to the same general project – that is, to identifying the material basis for women's oppression. All four understand that the task of identifying the sources of women's oppression includes a concern with methodology. The kinds of questions we ask and the way we proceed to answer them will shape the types of answers we come up with. However, because they approach the issue from different perspectives, their assessment of the utility of marxism differs.

Pat Armstrong and Hugh Armstrong "Beyond Sexless Class and Classless Sex: Towards Feminist Marxism" argue that the "sexless class" which has been a central concept of marxism must be rejected in favour of an analysis which fully appreciates both class and gender. They review the literature on domestic labour, the one area where marxists have systematically attempted to develop such an analysis, claiming that through the domestic labour debate, marxists have "honed the analytical tools" and "laid the basis for an analysis that is more...conscious of sex divisions". To such an analysis they argue must be added an understanding of women's bodies and their reproductive capacities. The result they claim will be a "feminist marxism".

Angela Miles "Economism and Feminism: Hidden in the Household A Comment on the Domestic Labour Debate" disagrees with Armstrong and Armstrong's position. Instead she argues that while the domestic labour theorists *claim* to be explaining gender inequality, in fact the economism of their marxism obscures the insights of "feminist radicalism". She concludes by calling for "the initiation of an already too long delayed Marxist/feminist dialogue". Patricia Connelly "On Marxism and Feminism" reviews both of these articles, disagreeing sharply with Miles and contrasting the Armstrong and Armstrong argument with Michele Barrett *Women's Oppression Today*. Connelly presents a third way of approaching the problem which she maintains will lay "the basis for a Marxist-feminist analysis of specifically feminist questions".

This short collection should provide a succinct introduction to the Marxist/Feminist debate and provide the beginning guidelines for a more expanded study.

Meg Luxton
Toronto
April, 1985

Pat Armstrong and Hugh Armstrong

Beyond Sexless Class and Classless Sex: Towards Feminist Marxism

There can be little doubt that marxism has been and continues to be, as Heidi Hartmann[1] puts it, sex-blind. True, many journals and anthologies today include at least one article by women on women and much political economy now attaches a paragraph or two acknowledging the existence of women. But this paper is not an attack on discrimination in political economy or an appeal to pay more attention to women's issues. Rather it argues that marxism must recognize that sex differences are integral to all levels of theory and analysis. The issue is not "women's questions" or "the question of women" but the efficacy of an analytical framework which fails to recognize or explain how and why sex differences pervade every aspect of human activity.

Building on and profiting from a wide range of feminist and marxist analysis, the paper suggests ways to move beyond the classless sex of much feminist writing, and sexless class of most marxist work, to a political economy that recognizes sexual divisions as integral to theoretical development. Sex differences were hardly a central concern for the "fathers" of political economy, yet the analytical tools developed by Marx and Engels can help us explore the social construction of the fundamental divisions between men and women. In their initial discussion of the relation between production and reproduction, they laid the basis for such an analysis.

The domestic labour debate, out of fashion in recent years, did attempt to extend marxist analysis, in order to apply it to the question of women. Not surprisingly, given their pioneering nature, these early efforts were fraught with difficulties. Often mechanical, functionalist and undialectical in trying to relate women to the capitalist production process, these applications sometimes distorted marxist categories to the point of uselessness. Biological differences were rarely discussed; resistance seldom recognized; ideology frequently ignored. Nevertheless, by focusing on the historical development of the work which takes place outside the market and on the contribution of this labour to the accumulation process, the debate has exposed many of the mechanisms which divide the sexes and subordinate women. It has established the pervasiveness of sex segregation in all kinds of labour and the significance of work in the home for the daily and generational reproduction of free wage labourers. It has shown how market conditions to a large extent shape and are in turn shaped by domestic work. Unfortunately this crucial theoretical work seems to be largely invisible to much of political economy.

Through a critical evaluation of the insights and issues raised in this debate, the paper suggests ways to move towards a political economy that is sex conscious as well as class conscious — towards a feminism that is class conscious as well as sex conscious. Our purpose is to argue that sex divisions should be considered at all levels of analysis and to suggest that theoretical efforts should focus on developing an analysis of class that recognizes the fundamental cleavages based on sex and on an analysis of biology that is historical, materialist and dialectical. The capsule view presented here of the domestic labour debate is intended to illustrate that the development of such theory is itself a collective, dialectical and historical process. As Wally Seccombe[2] points out, "This can never be a merely additive process, like finding the long lost piece in a jig-saw puzzle and happily inserting it in the space left waiting for it." It requires a reworking of theory, not just an "adding on" of women to class analysis, not just an inserting of class differences into feminist approaches. This paper is meant as a contribution to the ambitious reworking project.

Marxist Analytical Tools
Our starting point in this project is — to use C. Wright Mills's term — that of plain marxists.[3] We seek to work within Marx's own tradition, which requires that we avoid treating his writing as a holy writ through which to search for the correct answers. The danger of creating a vulgar or dogmatic marxism is nowhere more apparent than in analyzing the position of women. Marx and Engels, most marxists would agree, did not say much about women, and what they did say is not always useful or illuminating both because they concentrated on

explaining capitalist production and because they reflected the particular male bias of their historical period. As Sheila Rowbotham[4] points out, "Despite the depth of their historical analysis, the range of their knowledge and the extent of the commotion their writing has helped to create, Karl Marx and Frederick Engels were still a couple of bourgeois men in the nineteenth century." Or, as Juliet Mitchell[5] puts it, "Raking around in the texts of the master under the heading 'women' is enough to convince the most loyal marxist that the founder was a male chauvinist *par excellence.*" But Mitchell goes on to say that it is a ridiculous task to search through Marx for a complete explanation of the situation of women, ridiculous because historical materialism is an approach, a method of analysis.

For us, it is a method that is materialist, dialectical and historical. By materialist, we understand an approach that posits the existence of a real material world, one which conditions the social, political and intellectual processes in general. At the same time, we seek to distance ourselves from the economic determinism that pervades so much of orthodox marxism and that has so frequently and justifiably been attacked by (among others) feminists of all persuasions. The ways people co-operate to provide for their daily and future needs, combined with the techniques and materials at their disposal, establish the framework within which all human activity takes place. This does not mean that everything can be reduced to or is determined by matter; nor does it imply that ideas are irrelevant, false or the mere products of material conditions. Central to dialectical materialism is the rejection of a false dichotomy between ideas and reality; indeed, of all such separations. Their very relatedness is central to the framework. "Human beings are not active in their productive life and consequently conscious in the remainder of their existence. They are conscious in their productive activity and active in the production of their consciousness."[6]

Marx of course went far beyond the call to begin with an analysis of material conditions. He exposed how capitalism became dominant, and isolated its motivating force, accumulation. In the insatiable drive for capitalist accumulation, more and more goods and services are bought and sold. Labour power, or the capacity to work, is itself increasingly transformed into a commodity, as more and more people are separated from alternative means of providing for their basic needs and have to rely increasingly on the purchase of wage goods. Because Marx understood that the commodity production process establishes the broad framework for any capitalist society, he initially focused on how this production process works. He, like the capitalists, left the reproduction of workers largely to themselves. But free wage labour, which is essential to the very definition of capitalism, entails the reproduction of labour power primarily at another location. This separation under capitalism between commodity production and human reproduction (including the reproduction of the commodity labour power) in turn implies a particular division of labour between the sexes, and thus a division within classes. It is a division that pervades all work, whether productive of surplus or not, and one which is fundamental to the understanding of how the capitalist production system operates at all levels of abstraction and of how and under what conditions people will rebel.

Two related points following from this line of argumentation need to be underlined. First, by agreeing with Marx to assign pride of place under capitalism to the commodity production process — to the process by which surplus value is produced and appropriated — we distinguish ourselves from those who advocate a dual systems approach, with structures of patriarchy assuming a weight equal to, or at least an independence from, those of capitalism. While acknowledging that the subordination of women pre-dates capitalism, we find that the term partriarchy tends to conceal more than it reveals about the many forms of this subordination. More light can be shed on the subordination of women by understanding it as inherent to the capitalist mode.

This leads to the second point, which is that we are able to use Marx's approach in moving beyond his sex-blind position. It is precisely by accepting his argument on the primacy of commodity production that we gain further insight into the subordination of women in capitalist society. We are not being reductionist or more specifically economistic to insist that wage labour is distinct from domestic labour. The logic of the capitalist accumulation process has made them distinct. Furthermore, it is capital, not (faulty) marxist analysis, that has devalued the domestic labour which is performed normally by women, and which in turn conditions their participation in wage labour.

At the same time, we should of course avoid being carried away by the apparently compelling logic of the system. Marxist analysis is not simply materialist; it is dialectical and historical as well. Just as "materialism" has a double meaning — that there is a real world and that material conditions establish the framework for any society — so too is "dialectical" used in two senses. For Marx, every system produces contradictions at all levels. Not only are capital and labour in constant conflict, but in the process of attempting to cope with this conflict, new contradictions are constantly being created, combatted and partially resolved, generating even more contradictions. At the same time, the term dialectical can also mean that social processes and social relations are in themselves contradictory. Seccombe provides an example by arguing that "Although the proletarian condition is formally an open one, the great mass of the class cannot escape its class position even though, as individuals, they are free to try."[7] Similarly, wage labourers are freely compelled under capitalism to sell their ability to work to an employer. So too are women freely compelled to marry and to have children, and thus to do domestic work and, under certain conditions and within certain limits, labour-force work as well.

With his eyes fixed too firmly on the commodity production process, Marx was unable to incorporate the conflicts between women and men, and between households and capital, into his dialectical analysis. Nor was he able to perceive the contradiction in the free compulsion facing women, who cannot often be full participants in capitalist society unless they are wives and mothers, and cannot often be full participants if they are. His view of contradiction, and thus of struggle, was partial and flawed. While the working class may or may not be differentiated by race, ethnicity, religion, occupation, industry or whatever, it is invariably differentiated by sex. It is perhaps not accidental that for Marx, it is *men* who make their own history, albeit not under conditions of their own choosing. The standard worker was for him at best sexless, at worst always male. As a result, the orthodox marxist view of class struggle is vitiated by the failure to recognize that the working class has two sexes, a failure which hinders the understanding of men, much less of women.

The recognition that the working class has two sexes need not be the grounds for pessimism about the working class as revolutionary agent. After all, the working class household can be an expression of unity as well as of tension between the sexes. More importantly, the seeds of pessimism are sown above all by failure, and an aspect of any successful working class struggle to create itself is that it must become conscious of itself — a development which entails taking into account its own contradictions. Ignorance is not bliss, at least not for long. So the fact that sex differences cannot be eliminated by an effort of will is of tremendous strategic importance. We can agree with marxism that the subordination of women is certain to continue as long as capitalism continues. We would add that the demise of the capitalist accumulation process will not necessarily mean an end to the subordination of women, and further that if the revolutionary project is limited to the elimination of this process, it is unlikely to attract many women to its banner. Nor should it. The strategic point then, is to stretch dialectical analysis to make it a better tool for understanding and changing reality, for men as well as for women, for women as well as for men.

All these material conditions, contradictions and struggles have a history. In insisting on historical development, Marx was emphasizing the social construction of reality at the same time as he was drawing attention to the wide range of possibilities that exist within any particular mode of production and within any social formation. Where the capitalist mode is dominant, it transforms all aspects of society. Money, class differences, the sexual division of labour — they all predate capitalism, but all acquire a different significance and form under this mode. None, however, remains untouched by the logic of the dominant mode. There are necessary conditions for capitalism, but these can be satisfied in a number of ways. Yet the very workings of capitalism are modified by the struggles both to impose certain capitalist possibilities as against others and to transcend (or to maintain) the capitalist mode itself. Indeed, many of the practices and ideas that develop under capitalism are contrary to the interests of capital. So analysis must be historical as well as dialectical and materialist. It must sort out the historical variations between modes of production and within them. More concretely, it must distinguish what is central to the logic of the capitalist mode of production from what is within the range of possible capitalist variations. It is in this spirit that we reject both the ahistorical usage of the concept of patriarchy and assumptions about the unchanging nature of human biology.

With an approach that is materialist, dialectical and historical, it is possible to evaluate critically the domestic labour debate. In our view this debate is most fruitfully seen as starting with the first feminist efforts in the late 1960s to link the subordination of women to the sexual division of labour, and more specifically to relate domestic labour to wage labour. These efforts have involved but have not been restricted to considerations of value and domestic labour. Much of the debate has also centred usefully on questions of class and of strategy for women, and thus for men. The debate has helped make more transparent both the subordination of women and the workings of capitalism.[8] It is to an evaluation of the domestic labour debate, broadly conceived, that we turn next. As the debate has shifted to a new terrain, new directions for analysis have emerged. In particular, work needs to be done to make the analysis of human biology more materialist, dialectical and historical. We examine this issue in the concluding sections of the paper.

The Domestic Labour Debate

In 1890, Engels wrote that "Marx and I are ourselves partly to blame for the fact that the younger people sometimes lay more stress on the economic side than is due to it. We had to emphasize the main principle vis-à-vis our adversaries, who denied it, and we had not always the time, the place or the opportunity to give their due to the other elements involved in the interaction."[9] With the rebirth of feminism in the late 1960s, it is not surprising that, in attempting to provide a material explanation for women's subordination — in trying to counter those who understood women's oppression primarily in terms of the ideas in their heads or the hormones in their bodies — theorists concentrated on women's work and its usefulness to capitalism. Nor is it surprising given the centrality of class both to marxist analysis in general and to the struggle for change in particular, that marxists asking feminist questions began by trying to fit women into the class concept. These early explorations were thus frequently functionalist and reductionist, dismissing biology and dealing only peripherally with ideology. In the process, they sometimes distorted marxist categories, reducing their usefulness without making the subordination of women more transparent. The debate quickly became more refined, complex, and multi-dimensional, moving away from an exclusive focus on the movement of matter and away from the equally problematic approach of making women's subordination virtually autonomous from the workings of capitalism, as it tends to be in the dual systems theory. But the analysis continued in many ways to be undialectical. The inherent contradictions in positions taken are only now being explored. Neither resistance[10] nor biology[11] often arose in the debate — at least not on the marxist side. Women at best appear primarily as victims, at worst as being prepared to collude in their own oppression. It is time to put women back in their own history, to place the sexual division of labour at the centre, not the periphery, of marxist analysis. It is time to move beyond the domestic labour debate, by building on its contribution.

Whether it is Engels claiming that "The first class antagonism which appears in history coincides with the development of the antagonism between man and woman in the monogamous marriage, and the first class oppression with that of the female sex by the male,"[12] or Marx viewing class struggle as the major force for change, an early and continuing issue in marxist feminist analysis concerns the relationship of women to class.

Engels' statements in *The Origin of the Family, Private Property and the State* were ambiguous enough to form the basis for diametrically opposed approaches to understanding women and class. Shulamith Firestone, in what has stood up as a clear and comprehensive statement of the radical feminist position, commends Engels for observing that "the original division of labor was between men and women for the purposes of childbearing," although she also argues that "Engels has been given too much credit for these scattered recognitions of the oppression of women as a class." Nevertheless, she contends that marxism provides a method for a "materialist view of history based on sex itself," one that recognizes that women form a class by virtue of their shared biology. For Firestone, sex is class: "The natural reproductive difference between the sexes led directly to the first division of labor at the origins of class."[13] Like the productive technology which will lay the basis for equality in productive relations, scientific developments will free women from the tyranny of reproduction and childrearing, eliminating the physical differences between men and women and, not incidentally, the basis of all other differences amongst people as well. Such an approach is clearly ahistorical, denying that women's procreative and childbearing activities take place within a social context — one that is dominated, although not determined, by decisions and actions taking place in the market. Consequently, it also ignores the class differences amongst women, differences which have an important influence on the timing, experience and consequences for women of childbirth and childrearing. It fails to consider the way women have fought for, and gained, some control over their bodies. And the implication that the elimination of the biological differences between men and women will cause all other differences to wither away is difficult to consider seriously. Moreover, technology is not an independent force but one that is developed, introduced and sustained within a social context.

But the importance of women's procreative possibilities and childbearing responsibilities cannot be so easily dismissed. In searching through the cross-cultural and historical research, amongst the enormous variety in social formations and practices, only childbearing and infant care appear as common factors for women, suggesting that these realities play a significant role in women's subordination. While the historical and class variations in the process of childbearing, birth, and caring indicate that the productive factors alter the conditions for the meaning, consequences and experience of the procreative process, and that sex does not therefore make women a class, women's bodies clearly set them apart from men. The implications of these differences too have a history, and also vary with class, but they cannot be ignored in any class analysis.

Nevertheless, sex differences have seldom been acknowledged in marxist analysis that is not also feminist. Instead of classless sex, or sex as class, we have sexless class. When sex divisions are considered, they often appear as a kind of epiphenomenon, a result of the exclusion of women from capitalist production. Charnie Guettel, an early entrant in the struggle to apply marxist analysis to feminist questions, argued in *Marxism and Feminism* that "Women are oppressed by men because of the form their lives have had to take in a class society, in which men and women are both oppressed by the ruling class." She too contends that Engels "provides a basis for explaining the origins of women's subjection and, by extension, for discovering the conditions for their emancipation," although she also criticizes him for failing to "develop an analysis of women's oppression under capitalism" and for not mentioning "unequal pay and the responsibilities of maternity." Like Engels, she sees women's labour force participation and the collectivization of domestic labour as the prerequisites of women's liberation because "women's position within the contending classes determines her role in the struggle."[14] Since women's subordination is the result of capitalist organization, women must become wage labourers, become members of the proletarian class, and, as members of that class, struggle for change.

Like Firestone, Guettel finds support for her argument in Engels, but she arrives at the opposite conclusion that women do not form a class. Furthermore, the working class does not, or at least will not, contain fundamental sex divisions once there is "socialization of many of the childcare and domestic functions which are the material basis for women's inequality with men in the labour force."[15] By implication, sex differences will eventually wither away. Indeed, she argues that feminists have underestimated the extent to which they have already disappeared in socialist countries. This approach is also ahistorical in failing to acknowledge the male dominance that predates capitalism. To be sure, under capitalism all relationships are transformed, but in understanding their current nature it is important to examine the factors contributing to their precapitalist existence. Because she fails to examine the persistence of female subordination, blaming it solely on capitalism, she also ignores what women have in common — their bodies and their childbearing possibilities — and underestimates the significance of domestic labour. Thus the difficulties of overcoming the sex divisions within classes are minimized and reduced to equal pay for work of equal value, organizing the unorganized, and taxing corporations to pay for universal, democratically controlled day care. The relationship between men and women within capitalism is developed in a mechanical, undialectical fashion. Only sexless classes resist. Women's control over their bodies and their sexuality is not part of the project, nor is their procreative work integrated into the structure of capitalism. Although women's work in the labour force is the primary, almost exclusive focus of this analysis, thus at best giving a distant second place to sex divisions, at worst denying their fundamental existence, this approach does draw our attention to the importance of women's entry into wage labour — work that cannot be ignored in explaining what divides women from women and from men.

For radical feminists like Firestone, women's biologically-determined shared work experience in childbearing and childrearing makes them a class. For marxists like Guettel, women's capitalist-determined oppression melts into their future work in the labour force, work that will integrate them into an undifferentiated proletarian class. Neither of these approaches pays much attention to the household labour that has become the focus of the domestic labour debate and of other attempts to fit women into the class concept on the basis of this work.

It is difficult now to appreciate the impact of Margaret Benston's "The Political Economy of Women's Liberation" when it appeared in 1969. Although attacked and largely abandoned by later theorists, Benston's article set many of the terms for the domestic labour debate and was immensely popular at the time because it finally seemed to provide an analysis that grounded women's oppression in their current work. Benston argues that women are already workers and thus a class in the objective marxist sense of the term under the historically specific conditions of advanced capitalism. Using the marxist distinction between use value and exchange value, she maintains that women can be defined as the group of people who are responsible for the production of simple use values associated with home and family, working in the precapitalist home production unit. Unlike the paid work of men, which produces exchange value as well as use value, the unpaid work of women, which produces only use value, is valueless from the standpoint of capital. Although women might also participate in wage labour, such participation is transient and unrelated to the group definition. They form a reserve army of labour who can be called on when needed for capitalist production, and sent home when no longer required. This women's work is functional for capitalism because it fulfils "the needs for closeness, community, and warm secure relationships," and thus stabilizes the entire economy by maintaining the ideal consumption unit for capitalism — one in which the wages of the man purchase the necessary labour of two people, while allowing for the low-paid labour-force work of the woman as required. For Benston, there are two related material conditions for changing women's position. These are true equality in job opportunities outside the home, and the transfer of work now done in the home to the public economy. "Once women are freed from private production in the home, it will probably be very difficult to maintain for any long period of time a rigid definition of jobs by sex."[16] Nevertheless, she suggests that such changes would be difficult, if not impossible, under capitalism because the socialization of housework would require a massive redistribution of wealth, because women's unpaid labour is profitable and because the women released into the labour force could not be absorbed by it. Furthermore, ideas reinforcing women's inferiority will be difficult to change — indeed cannot change — without dramatic alterations in the structures that support them.

The argument is provocative, confusing and internally contradictory, yet it raises most of the issues that must be dealt with if we are to make the position of women understandable. She does suggest that capitalism has transformed the content and meaning of work, although she does not develop the argument. Cut off from the means of subsistence, money has become increasingly necessary to purchase what is needed for survival, but increasingly, can be acquired only by selling the ability to work for a wage. More and more goods and services are commodified, although much of domestic labour is not. The source of power and control is the market and it is this production for the market which relegates unpaid work to a secondary status that creates not only the definition of work but much of domestic work itself. Indeed, domestic work as a separate form of work does not predate capitalism. Yet Benston maintains both that capitalism defines women's work and that this work is precapitalist and preindustrial. She cannot have it both ways. While her distinction between use value and exchange value does expose the dominance of capitalism and does emphasize the fact the women too do work that is both useful and necessary, it does not establish domestic labour as a precapitalist form that will wither away.

The distinction does, however, allow her to introduce the concept of the reserve army of labour, although her definition of women's labour force work as transient, with no structural relation to capital, limits the usefulness of this approach for her. Nevertheless, the concept can be used, as Patricia Connelly has so clearly shown in *Last Hired, First Fired,* in order to "emphasize women's permanent connection to the production process," and to provide "a link between their labour force participation and their work in the home." According to Connelly's expansion of the analysis, "under advanced capitalist forms of production, not only does female domestic labour have no exchange value, but female wage labour receives less than its exchange value."[17] Since women do necessary work in the home which does not have exchange value, they form a cheap, available labour supply, competing with each other for women's segregated labour-force jobs in a way that not only keeps down their wages but those of men as well.

The distinction between use value and exchange value thus indicates how capitalism transforms work primarily into wage labour and domestic labour (making the latter invisible in the process), and allows an exploration of the relationship between the two through the concept of the reverse army of labour; it does not, however, solve the problem of how to fit women into the class concept. While Benston argues that women are now a class on the basis of their production of use values in the home, her conclusions suggest that women are to become part of another class by eliminating their household labour and joining the labour force on equal terms. What, then, is the use of declaring them a class by virtue of their household labour? And how can class differences amongst women be explained? Like Guettel, she seems to assume that sex distinctions will disappear when women join the working class.

While she does offer a material base for women's oppression, focusing exclusively on women's work and its uses to capitalism, Benston does not understand this work in dialectical terms nor does she see the structure as a result in part of struggles between men and women and between workers of both sexes and owners. Freely compelled to marry, freely compelled to mother, and now freely compelled to undertake labour force work, the essence of womanhood can be contradictory. The home is not simply a stabilizing force. The family is not simply created by capitalism. The home is filled with tensions that also result from developments within capitalism. Its existence depends to some extent on the efforts of male workers to obtain a family wage, on their struggles both to prevent women from competing for their jobs and to protect "the weaker sex," on women's attempts to decrease their workload and to maintain what is sometimes a haven, and on the nature of women's work itself, especially their procreative work.

But perhaps the most controversial legacy Benston bequeathed to the domestic labour debate was her statement that domestic labour is valueless from the standpoint of capital. Does domestic labour produce value? Is it subject to the law of value? What does this mean for the women's struggle and for the possibility of eliminating sex divisions within a capitalist society? Concern with these questions gradually shifted the debate away from the class issue towards a focus on the reproduction of labour power and the connection of women's work to capitalist production.

Peggy Morton, in her 1970 article, "Women's Work is Never Done," was the first to argue that it is necessary to "see the family as a unit whose function is the maintenance of the reproduction of labour power," that "this conception of the family allows us to look at women's public (work in the labour force) and private (work in the family) roles in an integrated way." This position also led her to reject the idea that women form a class on the basis of their work. Although shared domestic labour means that "real contradictions exist for women as women. . . . Women are nevertheless objectively, socially, culturally and economically defined and subjectively define themselves through the class position of their husband or their family and/or the class position derived from work outside the home."[18] Not only are there contradictions between both kinds of work; there are also inherent contradictions in the nature of the work in either place. The family does function for capitalism in socializing children, repressing sexuality and instilling appropriate hierarchical relationships through the education of future workers, but this is no smooth process. The very needs of the system create conflicting demands on the family, on women and on children, providing the basis for the development of strategy and militant struggle. Since male supremacy is structural, not just attitudinal, the struggle must be directed towards changing the structure of the system itself.

For Morton then, women do not simply produce use values; they produce something that connects them much more directly to capitalism — labour power. While she did not draw out the implications of this argument, and did not raise the question of value that was to become central to the later debate, she did develop a much more dynamic and dialectical approach to women's work, connecting women's domestic and wage labour, placing them within the contexts of capitalism and ideas about male supremacy, thus illustrating the contradictions that are inherent in this duality of domestic and wage labour. Recognizing the two workplaces of women and the class inequalities amongst women, she rejects the notion that women form a class. Not addressing directly women's shared procreative capacities, she raises, but does not explore, questions of women's control over their bodies and the class differences in access to birth control and abortion.

Other theorists, like Mariarosa Dalla Costa and Selma James,[19] adopted the argument that women are responsible for the maintenance and reproduction of labour power, but claimed that women constitute a class on the basis of this work in the home. Women are not to demand, as Benston argues, access to the same jobs as men. Instead they are to demand pay for the work they are now performing in the home. For these theorists, women now perform productive labour, that is, work that produces surplus value. The housework of women appears to be a personal service outside of capitalism, but it is in reality the reproduction of labour power, a commodity which is essential to the production of surplus value. The specific form of exploitation that this domestic work represents demands a corresponding specific form of struggle — namely the women's struggle — within the family. The family is at the core of the capitalist organization of work. It is a social factory. This recognition of the family as a centre of reproduction for labour power — as the other hidden half of capitalist organization and exploitation, and as the other hidden source of surplus labour — entails the recognition of the social power of women. Women must exercise this power by refusing to work, by demanding wages for housework, by throwing the responsibility for housework where it belongs — on capital. Thus the significance of defining women as a class on the basis of their domestic labour is that, as a class, they can become central to the class struggle in their own right.

But Dalla Costa and James misuse Marx's distinction between different kinds of labour. They confuse productive and unproductive labour. The purpose of any theory, and therefore its usefulness, rests on its ability to make transparent the opaque — to expose how the thing actually works. By applying to domestic labour categories that make capitalist production transparent frequently requires alteration in definitions and usage. The significance of altered usage does not, however, lie in its being an act of disloyalty to the arcane jargon of a century-old revolutionary. At issue is neither dogmatism nor the claim to be true to Marx. Rather, what is of significance is the capacity of Marx's careful distinctions to expose how capitalism works. Therefore, it is not only "Marxist purists," as Ann Oakley claims, who "need concern themselves with any epistemological uncertainty on this point."[20] It is anyone who wants to find out how and why women remain subordinate.

For Marx, productive labour under capitalism is labour that is exchanged directly (that is, for a wage) with capital in order to provide surplus value. Since housework is not directly exchanged with capital to produce surplus value, it is not in strict marxist terms productive, and those who do it are not exploited. By collapsing useful and productive labour into one category, Dalla Costa confuses the content of the product with the social relations involved in the labour — the usefulness of the activity in general with its specific social form. It was to avoid this confusion that Marx employed "useful labour" as an ahistorical concept denoting all labour that produces use value, and restricted "productive labour" to capitalism, an historically specific mode of production with, as a result, specific social forms. While all productive labour is also useful labour, not all useful labour is productive. Capitalism was for Marx the social formation in which exploitation normally takes the form of the exchange of commodities and in which labour power is normally bought and sold as a commodity. Thus the social form termed "productive labour," and defined as labour exchanged directly with capital to produce surplus value, is specific to capitalism because it is central to the very definition of capitalism. Without productive labour, there is no capitalism. Without the concept of "productive labour" and without the distinction between it and the concept of "useful labour," the laws of motion of the capitalist mode of production cannot be understood. Since a wide range of behaviour produces use values, to define domestic labour as the production of use values is not very illuminating either, since it merely puts it in the ahistorical category of work. Since only labour exchanged directly with capital in order to provide surplus value is productive in marxist terms, to define domestic labour as productive is simply confusing.

Furthermore, placing domestic labour in the category of productive labour does not, as other adherents to this argument maintain, affect its value. Indeed, defining domestic work as productive leaves no room to explain, as Benston does, why it has become invisible and devalued under capitalism. In addition, it leans towards an idealist explanation, suggesting not only that the cause of the invisibility is the labelling of domestic work as unproductive labour, but also that renaming will increase its value.

There is, perhaps, a more serious problem with this analysis. Paying women a wage would solidify the separation of women from men without altering substantially the nature and conditions of the work and without fundamentally challenging the structure of capitalism. Although some domestic work has already become commodified in the market, capitalism is premised on the very separation of the reproduction of the wage labourer from the productive process, and wages for housework may serve primarily to reinforce this necessary separation. The contradictory needs and processes that develop in capitalism and in women's work form no part of such an analysis — an analysis that leads to a strategy to sustain rather than challenge the subordinate position of women, especially when the analysis does not take explicit account of the nature of women's procreative work.

The argument that women, in providing the care and feeding of men and children, are performing work that produces surplus value shifted the focus of the debate from questions of class to questions of value, sparking a theoretical struggle waged to a large extent on the pages of *New Left Review*. In the initial article of this debate, Wally Seccombe argues that although domestic labour is not productive in the marxist sense, because it is not exchanged directly with capital to produce surplus value, it is nonetheless necessary under capitalism because the commodities bought for domestic consumption, and thus for the reproduction of labour power, have to be converted into their final form before they can be consumed.[21] For Seccombe, the character of domestic labour under capitalism is that it contributes simultaneously to the creation of the commodity labour power while having no direct relation with capital (that is, producing no surplus value). It thus creates value (as does any labour-producing part of a commodity) while not being subject to the law of value. Seccombe develops his argument by means of an analysis of the mystification inherent in the wage, which appears to be exchanged for the labour performed on the job site, but which in fact is exchanged for the labour needed to reproduce labour power. Since domestic labour is part of this labour to reproduce labour power, it creates value that is equivalent to the production costs of its maintenance, despite the fact that is does so under privatized conditions.

Alternative interpretations of the relationship between domestic labour and value arose in the debate. While arguing that domestic labour does not create value, Jean Gardiner maintains that it "does nevertheless contribute to surplus value by keeping down the necessary labour time, or the value of labour power, to a level that is lower than the actual subsistence level of the working class."[22] Housework, although not defined here as productive labour, does result in surplus labour and thus allows the "payment by the capitalist of wages below the value of labour power."[23] Since it lowers the value of labour power, it is necessary to the profits of the capitalist. But this position also became the subject of attack.

Essentially the criticisms of the argument that housework creates value boil down to the fact that domestic labour is not equivalent to wage labour. By claiming that housework creates value, these theorists must be suggesting that housework is itself a commodity that is exchanged for part of the husband's wage. Yet as Margaret Coulson et al. in particular point out, the housewife as housewife does not sell her labour power as a commodity to her husband.[24] Although she does contribute to the maintenance and reproduction of labour power, her participation in the social process is mediated by the marriage contract rather than the labour contract. She is not paid a wage: the exchange between husband and wife is variable and arbitrary, and subject to interpersonal bargaining. This has fundamental consequences in terms of the difference between wage labour and domestic labour. Wage labour is free labour in the sense that the wage labourer sells his labour power to an employer of his choice for a definite period of time in return for a wage. Time not at work is his own and he is free to change employers when he wishes (and conditions permit). The employer constantly attempts to decrease the necessary labour time, which is paid for in the form of a wage, in order to increase surplus value.

Domestic labour, on the other hand, is not free labour. For the housewife, there is little distinction, in terms of either time or space, between her work and her leisure. Since she is not paid a wage and thus does not produce surplus value directly, there is little interest on the part of the capitalist in reducing the necessary labour time by increasing her productivity. Since her work is based on social and emotional as well as economic commitments, it is difficult for her to change "employers" freely. And the relationship between husband and wife is different from that between employer and employee both because it is seldom a strictly economic relationship and because it involves all, **rather than** part of, the housewife's daily life. Finally, because the relationship is a binding one, there is no tendency towards the equalization of labour that occurs in capitalist commodity production.

Domestic labour and wage labour are not equivalent; they are not interchangeable. Marx revealed the mechanisms that affect a specific form of work — wage labour. These mechanisms do not however apply in the same way to domestic labour, precisely because it is not wage labour. As Paul Smith points out, domestic labour is not directly responsive to the price of labour.[25] It is performed even when its product cannot be sold. Because it is not subject to the law of value, there is no social mechanism to define the necessary tasks, no measure of value, and it is not equivalent to other forms of labour. To argue, as Seccombe does, that domestic labour "contributes directly to the creation of the commodity labour power while having no direct relation with capital,"[26] does little to expose the nature of the relationship between domestic labour and wage labour. According to Gardiner, "there appears to be no mechanism for the terms of sale of labour power to be determined by the domestic labour performed in its maintenance and reproduction."[27] Better housework is unlikely to result in a better wage.

But to argue, as Gardiner later does, that domestic labour lowers the value of labour power, does not make this relationship any more transparent.[28] Because wage labour and domestic labour are not comparable, "there is no basis for the calculation of the transfer of surplus labour-time between the two spheres unless the law of value is redefined."[29] Men married to women who are full-time housewives do not receive lower wages than men married to women who work full-time in the labour force, or men of similar age with no wives at all. In fact, the reverse relationship is more likely; women married to men who receive low wages are more likely to work for pay and thus do less housework. It would make more sense to argue that women entering the labour force who obtain wage work, lower the value of labour power by covering at least some of the costs of their own reproduction rather than having all these costs met out of the husband's wage. Even if the cost of domestic labour is hidden, it is still a cost, making it difficult to understand why, in value terms alone, capital would have an interest in maintaining domestic labour — especially when some of its goods and services could be transformed into commodities, thereby producing surplus value.

The early value debate virtually ignored women's wage labour, concentrating as it did on the reproduction of workers, all of whom seemed to be male. In responding to his critics, Seccombe argued that there is an average domestic labour time which can be defined as "that labour time necessary to convert the average wage into the average proletarian household, at the average price of wage goods." From this base, he argues that when real male wages fall, women can compensate for the decrease by either intensifying their housework or be entering the labour force to "supplement the family income."[30] The woman makes a "value trade-off" when she enters the market, compensating for the increased cost of the replacement of her domestic labour with her additional income. But the argument that domestic labour creates value does not, as Seccombe claims, explain movement from one form of labour to the other. If they are equivalent, why would a woman take on the other job? Wage labour and domestic labour are not equivalent. It is precisely because domestic labour is not wage labour that they are not interchangeable. Women cannot decide today that they will quit being pregnant so they can go out to work, but they can decide to stop washing the floor once a week and do it only once a month. There is no "exchangeability of labour time embodied in wage goods for domestic labour time,"[31] as Seccombe argues. While clearly some housework can be replaced by purchasing goods previously processed at home, most women do not replace their domestic chores with McDonald burgers and substitutes hired to clean the toilets and make the beds. They simply leave some work undone, do some work less often, and lower the quality of other labour — none of which suggests that there is necessary labour time involved or that this work constitutes average domestic labour time. Indeed, it is precisely because women are not creating value and are not directly subject to the law of value (because they do not produce surplus value) that they can form a reserve army of labour. It is because floors can go unscrubbed and beds unmade, and because they can vacuum less often, that they can in many cases enter the labour force. And it is because they cannot easily transform infant care and childcare into purchasable items that many women with small children provide a less flexible supply of labour.

But to argue that domestic labour does not create value or surplus value and is not directly subject to the law of value is not to argue that the law of value does not influence this work. Under capitalism, all labour is transformed, since the law of value impinges on most aspects of human activity. As Seccombe points out in a later article, the household is influenced by both the labour market and the retail market.[32] The household varies in response to wages and the demand for labour, as well as in response to the prices and availability of goods and services, by varying family size and the spacing of children; by varying the wage labour of men, women and children; by adjusting purchases; and by going into debt. Further, women do base their "decision" to take on a second job to a large extent on female wages, male wages, and the prices of the commodities their families need.

The debate over the law of value has not shown that women's domestic labour creates value, although it has made clear the fact that women do necessary work at home — work that is useful to capitalism in many ways. While it has not shown that the law of value directly governs the allocation of domestic labour, it has opened the door to an analysis which explores how the operation of the law of value in the market impinges on the household, influencing but not determining domestic labour time and content. In struggling through the implications of applying the law of value to domestic labour, the participants in the debate have revealed the opposite of what was initially intended. They have shown how domestic labour differs from wage labour. They have thus led the way to the argument presented here: that it is the different nature of domestic labour — its existence outside the law of value and the production of surplus value — that creates the flexibility and thus the possibility of domestic workers becoming a reserve army.

It should not be assumed, however, that domestic labour is completely flexible — that there is no minimum necessary labour in specific households. Toilets may go uncleaned but infants do have to be fed. Nor should it be assumed that women's movement in and out of the labour force is completely flexible and/or simply a matter of choice. Instead of arguing that women were forced out of the labour force in early capitalism and later pulled in and out at the whim of capital, it is necessary to examine, in an historically specific way, which women were entering and leaving, and under what conditions. Patricia Connelly's work indicates that in Canada married men and single women were the first to be forced into wage labour, the first to lose access to the means of directly producing for their needs, the first to have no alternative but to sell their ability to work for a wage.[33] As well, some married women, probably more than official statistics indicate, also worked for a wage from the earliest period, because they too had no alternative way to acquire food and clothes. However, it seems likely that in Canada at least, many married women had access to the means of producing directly for their own survival or of gaining income without entering the labour market. Not only did they have considerable necessary labour in the home which prevented them from searching for wage work, but they could also directly produce food, sew clothes, do laundry, take on boarders or do other domestic chores, without selling their ability to work for a wage. Such alternatives do not mean that most men earned a family wage, nor do they mean that women were completely or even primarily dependent on a male wage. What they do mean is that women were supporting their own reproduction in a way that allowed them to combine this work with the labour they had little chance of escaping — childbearing and caring responsibilities. More recently, married women have been losing access to the means of production and to alternatives to wage labour. Darning more socks, even if polyester socks could be darned, does not greatly affect family maintenance. The point in this — a recital which may seem very familiar — is that we have been looking at women's work upside down. Instead of seeing women's domestic work as substituting for the wage, we should be seeing the wage as what becomes necessary when, like men, they have no alternative means of providing for their own needs. We should question whether women have ever been dependent on a male wage and if so, which women — women from which classes. By analyzing domestic labour from this perspective, we will not only expose the class differences amongst domestic workers — not only trace the transformation and commodification of much domestic work — but also perceive the reduction in women's access to means of support. For larger and larger groups of women, the intensification of domestic labour that is central to Seccombe's argument is not an alternative.

Moreover, women's movement in and out of the labour force should not be understood as being simply functional for capital or as a passive response by women to labour market requirements. By drawing women into the labour force, capital may lower the value of labour power through competition and decrease the costs of reproducing workers by spreading them over more workers, but it also may create a crisis because not all people can be absorbed into paid employment. Capital also encourages tension in the home, for women and men, between women and men. In addition some groups of women, especially those with higher education and training, are fighting to enter the labour force and to abandon their domestic chores; others, especially those with small children, are struggling to escape the compulsion to work at those dull, low-paid, monotonous jobs that create for them the double day. Of course, the alternatives are structured by capitalism itself. Resistance is seldom powerful enough to win, but it does have an influence that cannot be ignored. Women do not passively respond to family or market demands. None of this is to deny that women form a reserve army of labour, especially as part-time and seasonal workers. However, it is to argue that from this perspective, married women are becoming less and less flexible as their alternatives to wage labour are reduced. It is also to argue that some classes of women are more flexible than others and that women are active in directing their labour. And, it must not be forgotten that all of this happens within the context of a society that encourages ideas about male dominance and that values independence and competition, although these values themselves vary from class to class.

This summary and evaluation of the domestic labour debate has been presented here for a number of reasons. First, it is intended to illustrate that while the analysis was frequently mechanical and functionalist, and usually ignored resistance and biology, it did open the door to an approach that is historical, materialist and dialectical. We seek to expose not only the significance of domestic labour and its relation to wage labour, but also the variable, complex and dialectical development of this work. Through this exposition, it is possible to see the tensions created by the drive for accumulation — for commodification — and the resistance, based on these tensions, that have altered work in the home and in the labour force.

Second, this review is designed to illustrate the centrality of domestic labour and sex divisions to capitalism, to wage labour, and therefore to our theorization of how capitalism operates. Based on sex, separated from production, but conditioned by and in turn conditioning the market, domestic work is both intimately connected to, and a factor in, capitalist processes. Because domestic labour is not wage labour, women form a reserve army for the capitalist productive system. Because wage labour has become dominant and necessary — either directly or indirectly — to the survival of most people, other work and other workers have been devalued. Because domestic work is centred on the reproduction of the next generation of workers, as well as on the daily maintenance of all workers, it is women's work. Finally, this critical summary provides a basis for the next sections of this paper — sections which suggest ways to go forward in developing a political economy that comprehends the fundamental importance of sex divisions at all levels of analysis. The focus is on class, on the separation of domestic and wage labour, and on biological questions as central, but not the only, questions for a sex-conscious theory.

Sex is a Marxist Issue

Although feminists have focused on domestic labour, or the split between the public and the private, marxists who are not feminists have concentrated of the production process. If justified at all, this concentration on production is explained either in terms of the dominance of this process or in terms of the level of abstraction. At the highest level of abstraction, it is argued, sex divisions are irrelevant.

But, at the highest level, capitalism is defined as a system which separates capital from labour, with labour power typically bought and sold as a commodity. As Seccombe has so clearly explained, capitalism is premised on the existence of free wage labour.[34] The split between the public and the private is the very essence of capitalism. The sale of labour power as a commodity seems to assume reproduction at home, away from labour force work. It does not, of course, necessitate a particular kind of home or a particular kind of family. The nature and conditions of workers' reproduction are matter for historical investigation at another level of analysis. This does not however seem to be the case for the existence of the sexual division of labour itself, which necessarily accompanies the separation of the reproduction of labour power in some kind of home from the production of goods and services in some kind of market. Women, not men, have the babies. If producing the next generation of workers is separated from the commodity production of goods and services, then this split implies a division of labour by sex. The particular duties that are associated with procreation are matters of history, but the division is central to capitalism itself. It is no accident of history that the everyday tasks of maintaining and reproducing the next generation of workers have in fact been disproportionately performed by women.

There is a tendency within capitalism towards commodification; much of domestic labour has already been commodified. But it seems likely that there are real limits to this process if capitalism, and the free wage labourer, are to continue to exist. Some childcare work can be, indeed has been, integrated into the market economy. This labour can be equalized and abstracted. But babies can be produced only by fertile women. Such labour, at least given present circumstances, cannot therefore be equalized and abstracted. If all aspects of the reproduction of workers could be commodified, the process would require either the private production of workers with its consequent tendency towards monopoly (a circumstance inimical to the production of a free wage labourer), or an enormous expansion of the state (an eventuality counter to the existence of capitalism). Furthermore, the ideology of the free wage labourer, so important to the capitalist status quo, would be difficult to maintain if people were entirely produced through capitalist production processes or the state. A capitalist society, with its concomitant free wage labourer, seems to imply a separation, in some form, between the reproduction of workers and the production of goods and services. The separation seems also to imply a segregation, and denigration, of women.

Therefore, to insist on distinguishing a highest level of abstraction that entirely excludes consideration of a sexual division of labour is to be sexist — to reinforce the notion of women being hidden from history, or more accurately, from theory. It is also to guarantee an inadequate understanding of capitalism, given that the split between the public and the private, and thus a sexual division of labour, is essential to this mode of production, at the highest level of abstraction. In summary, the existence of a sexual division of labour, although not its form or extent, is crucial to capitalism and therefore to its theorization.

Class is a Feminist Issue

Few would deny that capitalist societies are class societies or that women as a group are oppressed. But the questions of whether or not there is a material basis to that oppression and of whether or not that basis is shared bodies or shared work is still a matter of debate. Are the fundamental divisions those between owners of the means of production and owners of labour power, those between men and women, or those between women and their bodies? Is the main enemy, to use Christine Delphy's terminology, capitalism, men or female anatomy?[35]

While it is essential for a class analysis to locate women in relation to class, the answer cannot be one of these alternatives alone. Women are simultaneously subject to capitalism, male dominance and their bodies. To pose the question in the form of alternatives is like asking whether ideas or material conditions structure women's subordination. They are inseparable. They act together. Patriarchy and capitalism are not autonomous, nor even interconnected systems, but the same system. As integrated forms, they must be examined together.

This is not to argue that women constitute a class. Although it is clear that most of those who own and control the means of production are male, most men own only their ability to work. There are also class differences amongst women. Lady Astor is not oppressed by her chauffeur and it is questionable whether her cleaning woman is more oppressed by her husband than her employer. Theorists have concentrated on exposing what women have in common, but not all theorists have ignored or dismissed class differences amongst women. Early in the domestic labour debate, Morton maintained that there were class differences amongst women — differences based on the class position of their husbands, their families, or their own labour force work. Roberta Hamilton explored the different work experiences and life situations of women in peasant, craft, "tradesman," and noble families in the transition to bourgeois and proletarian households.[36] Situating women within the family, and the family in turn within the dominant mode of production, Dorothy Smith argued that capitalism changed all women's work into a personal service but that there is a crucial difference between working class and middle class families. "The household for the working class woman is a means to meeting the needs of its members, and that is her work. Middle class women are oriented by contrast to the values and standards of an externalized order."[37] Bonnie Fox also distinguished between working class and middle class women — in this case on the basis of household income and resources.[38] The oppression takes different forms for these women. The consequences, nature and responses to male dominance vary from class to class.

To argue that there are class differences amongst women and that they do not form a class on the basis of their bodies or their work is not to solve the problem of fitting women into classes. Locating women through their domestic labour either puts most women into the same class or places them automatically in the same class as their husbands. For those women with direct involvement in the labour market, the alternatives are independent class membership, the same class membership as their husbands, or a common membership with other women because of the domestic labour they also perform. Gardiner's alternative of expanding the definition of the working class to include all those not directly involved in but dependent on the sale of labour power does expose the broad class cleavages but fails to take into account the fundamental divisions between men and women in the working class.[39] Surely having an indirect, rather than a direct, relationship to production has important consequences for women's class sympathies — sympathies which cannot easily be equated with those of the young and unemployed whose dependency is temporary and transient. Furthermore, such an approach ignores the double work of women, their position as a particular kind of reserve army, their segregation into separate labour force jobs, and the ideology that reinforces and is reinforced by these divisions.

The problem here is more than one of counting, of figuring out how to classify women. Both bourgeois and marxist categories treat sex differences as irrelevant to stratification and class systems. As Delphy points out, both approaches imply that "wider inequalities have no influence on the (assumed) 'equality' of the couple, and on the other hand that relationships within the couple because they are seen as equal cannot be the cause of wider inequalities."[40] Theories that lump all women together as a class ignore class differences amongst women. Theories that attach women to their husbands or families ignore women's subordination, their domestic labour and their labour force work. Theories which locate women in terms of their own paid employment forget both the segregation of the labour force, and the domestic labour that most women perform. Theories that are blind to sex differences obscure not only divisions fundamental to all classes, but also the structure of capitalism. The working class, as well as the ruling class, has two sexes. Without acknowledging these divisions — without integrating them into a class analysis — neither capitalism nor households can be understood. This is not a plea to add women back in, but a challenge to a theory that has not made the system transparent, has not developed an analysis of class which accounts for a bifurcation of classes — a division which is central to an understanding of how capitalism itself works.

The domestic labour debate does lay the basis for a revision of theory based on an expansion of the class concept. Without denying that the most basic divisions are between those who own and control the means of production and those who own only their labour power — a primacy implied by the dominance of the wage system in capitalist society — it is possible to comprehend the antagonisms between the sexes, and amongst those of the same sex, by including all labour in our analysis. Those dependent directly or indirectly on the wage are objectively and subjectively divided by their material conditions, by their lived experiences, and by the work they do. If work for a wage (or the absence of work for a wage) and work required to transform that wage into consumable form, as well as work necessary to provide the next generation of workers, are included in our approach to class, then divisions between men and women and amongst women may be better understood. Such an approach would permit the domestic and wage labour of both men and women to be taken into account. Domestic labour would thus form an integral part of the explanation for men's interests just as wage labour would be a basic component in comprehending women's class position and relations. Connecting domestic and wage labour within classes would also extend the analysis to the relationship between domestic and wage labour — to the sex segregation in both areas of work. In this way, it would be possible to develop a theory which exposes the material basis of the subjective and objective antagonisms between sexes. The domestic labour debate suggests a movement in this direction; marxism provides the tools; political economy should continue the work.

Bodies in History

For Marx, analysis at all levels should begin with the way people provide for their daily and generational needs — with the production and reproduction of goods, services and people. These production and reproduction processes are inseparable aspects of the same whole. They are social processes requiring co-operation, and are subject to historical change. They do however have physical components which set limits on possible variations. A minimum of food is necessary, some protection from the elements is essential, and some ejaculation, insemination and gestation must take place for babies to be born. While there are enormous variations in how physiological and socially constructed needs are satisfied, in all societies and throughout history, women have the babies.

That women have babies is not a matter which has relevance only at the level of a particular social formation. How women have babies, and the conditions and consequences of childbearing, are relative to particular social formations. So is the sexual division of labour related to childrearing. But the fact that women, not men, have babies is not. To theorize production and reproduction at the highest level of abstraction involves a recognition of the differences in female and male reproductive capacities. Any other approach fails to comprehend the nature of production and reproduction.

Here, we are distinguishing ourselves from much of marxist analysis. As Hamilton points out, "It is hard not to conclude that the effect of biological differences on the position of women is an embarrassment to marxists, that it is more or less known information which, like the happenings in a Victorian bedroom, is best left unexplored."[41] Those marxists who fail to discuss the sexual division of labour at all must be assuming, like Guettel, that it is a mere byproduct of the capitalist system and thus will wither away with the end of the system — that it is a minor factor in the functioning of capitalism. Those who discuss the sexual division of labour without acknowledging the biological component seem to point in a similar direction. Or perhaps they are assuming that procreative capacities are not amenable to marxist analysis. But this analysis must be extended to include sexuality, childbearing and childbirth if the realities of production and reproduction are to be understood and changed in a way that would benefit both women and men.

To recognize that women have the babies is not, however, to resort to a biological explanation of women's subordination, nor to call for the elimination of women's childbearing responsibilities. Unlike many feminists, we do not see biology as fixed and immutable. We do not see childbearing as the same for all women in the same society or in different historical periods. We do not see biological factors as primary or even separate factors. Physical capacities do not exist outside — autonomously from — power structures and productive processes. Nor are they beyond human control and manipulation. Procreation is itself to a large extent socially constructed. It has a history. Its process, its consequences, and its meanings also vary from class to class. Capitalism has transformed the productive and reproductive processes. Contradictions are created, resolved, and transformed. And women, on the basis of these contradictions, struggle to resist, to gain some control over their biological capacities. What follows is an indication of the direction a marxist analysis should take if it is to include women's particular reproductive capacities — in other words their procreative capacities — in the comprehension of production and reproduction in general.

It may be readily agreed that inequality results, not from the different biological capacities but from the social mechanisms which ensure that these capacities become a weakness rather than a resource. To suggest, however, that the very "biology" of the procreation process has varied historically with the economic system may be more a matter of debate. According to Gayle Rubin, "The needs of sexuality and procreation must be satisfied as much as the need to eat, and one of the most obvious deductions which can be made from the data of anthropology is that these needs are hardly ever satisfied in any 'natural form,' any more than are the needs for food."[42] Or as Richard Wertz and Dorothy Wertz put it in their history of "lying-in" in the United States: "Because people have understood and shaped birth in changing ways, both the means and the meaning of childbirth have a history, an extraordinary one because childbirth is at once a creative act, a biological happening, and a social event."[43] Research on the history of women's role in procreation clearly indicates that the general economic situation, the class structure, the development of technology, women's other work, health care and standards and available food supplies — in short, the economic system — affect the kind of pregnancies women go through, the number of pregnancies they have and their chance of survival.

For example, Louise Tilly and Joan Scott[44] show how low standards of nutrition and health in early modern England inhibited conception, promoted miscarriage, affected the milk supply of mothers and made women infertile by the age of forty or forty-five. Wertz and Wertz report that, in the colonies, as in France, "there was a seasonal periodicy to the arrival of children" which "may correlate not only with work demands and consequent exhaustion but also with nutritional variation."[45] In the introduction to her moving collection of English working class women's testimonials on their experiences with maternity, Margaret Davies argues that the high infant mortality rate and the extensive maternal suffering at the turn of the century were attributable to: (1) inadequate wages; (2) lack of knowledge regarding maternity and of skilled advice and treatment; and (3) the personal relation of husband and wife.[46] Similarly Neil Sutherland, referring to a 1910 report prepared for the Ontario government, lists the following as agents of high infant mortality rates:

> poverty, ignorance, poor housing, overcrowded slums, low wages and other social conditions that forced mothers of young children to work outside their homes, impure water and milk, loose controls over the spread of communicable diseases, poor prenatal care, inadequate medical attendance at birth, tardy registration of births, and the lack of clinics and nursing services helping mothers care for their babies properly.[47]

These factors, which also affect the process of pregnancy and childbearing, result primarily from the existing material conditions. And the very "biology" of menstruation also varies with these conditions over time. According to Janice Delaney, Mary Jane Lupton and Emily Toth, "the fact is, the age at menarche (first menstruation) depends greatly on good food and good health. Those who eat well mature earlier. Today, the average American girl first menstruates when she is twelve and a half years old. Figures from Norway, where the oldest such records are kept, show that in 1850 the average girl had her first period at seventeen; by 1950, at thirteen and a half. For each generation since 1850, then, a girl's period has come about a year earlier than her mother's."[48] Furthermore, as Joyce Leeson and Judith Gray point out, changes in economic and social arrangements have meant that "Thirty-five years or more of virtually uninterrupted menstruation is thus a recent phenomenon."[49] Bodies are not independent of their economic and social surroundings. The conditions are set by the productive system.

Yet changes in the productive system, and more specifically in women's work, do not automatically produce changes in women's experiences with sex and with childbearing. To quote Stella Browne, a socialist feminist writing in 1922, "No economic changes would give equality or self-determination to any woman unable to choose or refuse motherhood of her own free will." As she so eloquently explained: "Birth control for women is no less essential than workshop control and determination of the conditions of labour for men. . . . Birth control is woman's crucial effort at self-determination and at control of her own person and her own environment."[50] The development of, and the conditions of access to, birth control and abortion technology are clearly of central importance to women.

Some form of birth control has been known since hunting and gathering societies. Yet even the early forms were suppressed if and when this suited the interests of the productive system. As Linda Gordon argues, the coincidence of the suppression of birth control with the development of agriculture is attributable to the need for more labour power and the desire to control inheritance of the accumulating private property.[51] While new technology has been developed in the productive sector, religious and state laws have limited access to, and information on, both old and new methods of birth control and abortion.[52] The research carried out by Wertz and Wertz indicates that the technology and its regulation have had both positive and negative consequences for women.[53] The point is that the interests of women have seldom been taken into account in decisions to develop and to allow access to the technology; consequently, women have had difficulty in asserting control over their bodies through contraception and abortion technology.

Important as this technology and its regulation are to women, there are other ways in which their procreative experiences are conditioned by the productive and state sectors. Procreation is influenced by labour force demands, by state policies and regulations, and by economic requirements and resources. For instance, Tilly and Scott argue that "young populations and job opportunities for young workers kept birth rates from falling" in some French industrial cities during the mid-nineteenth century.[54] According to Angus McLaren, "Factory work often prevented the young mother from being able to nurse her child" in nineteenth-century England, thus reducing even the limited contraceptive protection provided by breast-feeding and consequently encouraging women to seek methods of abortion to prevent birth.[55] The "combination of large-scale immigration from Southern Europe and the casualities of the First World War stimulate[d] widespread alarm over birth and mortality rates,"[56] and resulted in government and private programmes designed to change the conditions of childbirth and childrearing. In 1937, when depression conditions had dramatically increased unemployment, the Canadian rate of natural increase dropped to a record low of 9.7 (per 1000 population) in spite of the restrictions in access to birth control techniques and information. During and immediately after World War II, the rate rose steadily from 10.9 in 1939 to a record high of 20.3 in 1954.[57]

In addition, these rates are affected, as many social policy researchers indicate, by existing laws and regulations which "touch on the ability to more effectively plan the number and timing of children by Canadian families (which will bring into consideration abortion and sterilization and contraception), the ability to determine the grounds on which individuals can decide to form or dissolve families (which will involve divorce laws and regulations), and the legal implications of the formation or dissolution of a family unit."[58] Today in Canada it is evident that the demand for women as workers in the labour force and the concomitant decline in the economic resources of the family have encouraged women both to participate in the labour force and to reduce the number of children they produce. This reduction itself has been made possible both by the development of birth control technology and by changes in state intervention — especially in the laws that relate to birth control and abortion, but also more generally in the provision of health care services and information.

Like the concept of the virgin mother, procreation has internal contradictions for women. Adrienne Rich has described in eloquent detail the contradictions inherent in mothering within an advanced capitalist society.[59] It is at one and the same time a joyful and painful experience. Women can see the possibility for control over their reproductive capacities, but the control is denied by abortion laws, poor technical development, medical practices and limited information, not to mention the ideology of male superiority. They have "free choice" in marrying and bearing children, but like the wage worker who is freely compelled to sell labour power, women are compelled by conditions of pregnancy, wage work, medical techniques and legal restrictions to marry and have babies in particular ways. Labour force work interferes with pregnancy and birth; pregnancy and birth interfere with labour force jobs.

And while capitalists seek to pursue their interests, the results are frequently contradictory here too. The process is dialectical. Barbara Ehrenreich and Deirdre English explain that Margaret Sanger's campaign for birth control in the United States was aimed at preventing the problems created by "overbreeding" in the working class.[60] But the consequence of her victory was a greater decline in the birth rate amongst those Sanger would have described as fit. In Canada, a Crown Attorney claimed in 1901, "that employment opportunities permitted women to avoid marriage or to fall back on 'crime' which led to a 'low birth rate'."[61] Women have more recently responded to the growth in demand for women workers and the rising costs of rearing children by reducing the number of children they have and by demanding childcare facilities. Now that the demand for female workers is falling off, there are few children to draw women back into the home, although decreasing support for existing childcare service increases the pressure on women to go back home.

More generally, the contradiction between the technical possibility for women to control their bodies and the lack of control which results from policies designed for other interests has formed the basis of women's protests for centuries. As Gordon points out in her history of birth control in America, "In no area of life have women ever accepted unchallenged the terms of service offered by men. Sexuality and reproduction were no exception."[62] There are many instances of such rebellion. McLaren argues that in nineteenth-century England, "the workers, and in particular the women workers of the textile areas, should be seen, not as waiting passively for the knowledge to trickle down from their superiors which would permit them to emulate the middle class, but as taking independent action, which might well violate bourgeois morality, in an attempt to achieve their own desired family size."[63] In Canada, "A contributor to the *Canadian Churchman* (1900) went so far as to assert that the pressures of existing society encouraged ' . . . to put it bluntly, in nine cases out of ten, women to murder their unborn children.' "[64]

The entire history of abortion indicates women's resistance to both the law and their procreative capacities. And similar patterns appear in breastfeeding practices. Reporting to the Ontario government in the early part of this century, Dr. Helen MacMurchy argued that women should be convinced to breastfeed their infants in order to prevent high infant mortality rates. "In order to encourage women to breastfeed, a mother's qualms about the cost of such a procedure had to be overcome. A working mother who could not adjust her schedule to a breastfeeding schedule should have a pension, if necessary, to take care of the family."[65] Women have not passively accepted the dictates of the state, the church, or men. Indeed, childbearing itself may be a form of resistance against imposed standards and against powerless conditions. Women may gain power from bearing children — power over children and over men. It should not be seen only as a passive response. Women are not merely vessels. They are active in making their own history.

In various historical periods, women's bodies, and their lack of control over their bodies, have provided the basis for the organized opposition of some women. But, while shared physiology has brought some women together, the variation created by existing material conditions has divided women — has encouraged women in different classes and in different marital situations to experience their bodies in different ways. Women differ in terms of the healthcare they receive during pregnancy, in terms of their access to information on birth control and on the way their bodies function, and in terms of the ease of gestation as it is related to nutrition, information and exercise. They also differ in the consequences of childbearing — whether it will cause financial or emotional strain, and whether it will limit free movement and/or labour force participation. Lady Astor and her maid may both give birth, but the treatment they receive and the consequences of childbirth for them vary greatly. This is clearly indicated by the research on women of different class positions. For instance, Ehrenreich and English show that, in nineteenth-century America, "It was as if there were two different species of females. Affluent women were seen as inherently sick, too weak and delicate for anything but the mildest pastimes, while working class women were believed to be inherently healthy and robust. The reality was very different. Working class women, who put in long hours of work and received inadequate rest and nutrition, suffered far more than wealthy women from contagious diseases and complications of childbirth."[66] Wertz and Wertz[67] describe how poor women were encouraged to deliver in hospitals so that doctors in training could practice on them. On the other hand, in Canada during the latter half of the nineteenth century, "one of the main reasons for the incidence of puerperal insanity [the 'insanity of childbirth'] in the Victorian era was, ironically, a consequence of medical practitioners delivering babies — a service which the well-to-do were more likely able to afford . . . . Today, it is evident that puerperal insanity had less to do with the nature of women than it had to do with the nature of medical treatment."[68] The letters from working-class English women collected by Davies at the turn of the century clearly indicate the "different conditions under which the middle-class and the working-class woman becomes a mother."[69] These examples suggest that there is not one procreative process for all women but different procreative processes for women in different classes and in different historical periods.

The alternative analytical approaches are not limited to ignoring sex differences, assuming they are mere social constructs, or concluding that they represent fixed, primary differences which create their own relations — ones which are beyond marxist analysis. An historical materialist approach not only allows us to situate female sexuality and childbearing within capitalism but also to show how these processes are conditioned within particular social formations — in different ways for women of different classes. It permits the integration of biological factors as limiting but not determining. Any alternative to capitalist organization must recognize that women, not men, have babies. Like other aspects of the material conditions which human beings face, the goal is to bring procreation under human control, to shape the conditions under which it happens. Theory in political economy should help us understand what these conditions are and how they can be changed; it should direct us towards a strategy to ensure that female bodies, like the ability to do work, are a resource rather than a liability.

That women have the babies, albeit under a variety of conditions, does not necessarily mean that they will rear the children or clean the toilets. Nor does it mean that they must live in nuclear families. However, because capitalism is premised on the separation of most aspects of workers' reproduction from the commodity production process, and because women have the babies, women will at times be limited in their access to the production process. Such limitations permit the elaboration of the sexual division of labour (itself not without contradictions) just as they encourage women's dependence on men for financial support and the dependence of higher-paid, wage-earning men on women for domestic services. Access to wage labour is value laden, given the primacy of productive processes and the centrality of the wage. Of course, precisely how this division comes about is a matter of historical investigation, beyond the scope of this paper.[70] But the domestic labour debate and other research suggest that such an approach can expose the mechanisms at work which ensure women's subordination.

Conclusion

The domestic labour debate has honed the analytical tools, has exposed the dual nature of women's work, has shown how this work is useful to capitalism and in the process has laid the basis for an analysis that is more dialectical, more historical, more conscious of active resistance, more conscious of sex divisions. Feminist analysis has shown that bodies and their procreative capacities also condition possibilities, although marxist analysis helps us to place these bodies in history, in classes, in relationships that are themselves best understood within the context of existing material conditions. In summarizing and evaluating the domestic labour debate, as well as in offering an alternative approach to understanding biological processes, this paper attempts to create a platform on which to build a critique of political economy and a sex-conscious analytical framework.

We have argued that there is a sexual division of labour particular to capitalist society (although many aspects clearly predate capitalism), that this division and the concomitant subordination of women are integral parts of capitalist production and reproduction and that this division has a biological component which cannot be ignored. Moreover, we argue that because capitalism is premised on free wage labour — on the separation of most aspects of workers' reproduction from the production process — women's reproductive capacities separate them out of the production process for childbearing work. This establishes the basis for an elaboration of sex differences, a sexual division of labour which subordinates women and pervades all levels of human activity under capitalism. Such segregation also fundamentally divides classes.

Any theory of capitalism must be conscious of and provide explanation not only for the separation between home and work but also for that between women and men. It must put women and men back into their history at all levels of analysis. The domestic labour debate suggests that marxist analytical tools can be applied to the task. That political economy has been sex blind is a challenge, not an indictment.

NOTES

*As Roberta Hamilton would say, like all publications this is only a draft gone public. Many people have provided critical comments on earlier drafts, and while few may still recognize the current paper, and while fewer still may want to be linked with it, we would like to thank Jacques Chevalier, Patricia Connelly, Roberta Hamilton, Jared Keil, Angela Miles, George Mitchell, Mary O'Brien, Shirley Pettifer, Wally Seccombe, Dorothy Smith, Pam Smith, Erica Van Meurs and Bonnie Ward in particular.

1. Heidi Hartmann, "The Unhappy Marriage of Marxism and Feminism: Towards a More Progressive Union," in *Women and Revolution,* ed. Lydia Sargent (Boston 1981), 2

2. Wally Seccombe, "Domestic Labour and the Working-Class Household," in *Hidden in the Household: Women's Domestic Labour Under Capitalism,* ed. Bonnie Fox (Toronto 1980), 27

3. C. Wright Mills, *The Marxists*, (New York, 1962), 98

4. Sheila Rowbotham, *Women, Resistance and Revolution* (New York 1974), 62

5. Juliet Mitchell, "Marxism and Women's Revolution," *Social Praxis* 1:1 (1972), 24

6. Richard Lichtman, "Marx's Theory of Ideology," *Socialist Revolution* 23 (1975), 51

7. "Domestic Labour," 53. (See n.2 above.)

8. The domestic labour debate itself may seem to have waned in recent years, replaced by a post-Althusserian concern with the autonomy of "patriarchy" and "patriarchal structures." Yet the debate is still powerful enough to have provoked a sustained attack by Christine Delphy and Diana Leonard at a plenary session of the most recent British Sociology Association meetings in Manchester, April 1982.

9. Frederick Engels, "Letter to J. Bloch in Konigsberg," in K. Marx and F. Engels, *Selected Works in Three Volumes,* vol. 3 (Moscow 1970), 488

10. Of course, the treatment of individual women resisting is common in feminist literature and art. See, for example, Judy Chicago's dazzling sculpture, "The Dinner Party." There has also been some discussion of the suffragette struggles and of women in trade unions, but there has been too little integration of these forms of resistance into a broader framework.

11. Certainly biology has been discussed by some feminists claiming to use a marxist analysis — notably Shulamith Firestone in *The Dialectic of Sex* (New York 1970) — but most marxists ignore the question.

12. Frederick Engels, *The Origin of the Family, Private Property and the State* (Moscow 1968), 66

13. *Dialectic of Sex,* 4, 5, 9. (See n.11 above.)

14. Charnie Guettel, *Marxism and Feminism* (Toronto 1974), 2, 8, 13, 36

15. Ibid., 58

16. Margaret Benston, "The Political Economy of Women's Liberation," reprinted in *Voices from Women's Liberation,* ed. Leslie Tanner (New York 1971), 285, 287

17. M. Patricia Connelly, *Last Hired, First Fired* (Toronto 1978), 6, 33

18. Peggy Morton, "Women's Work is Never Done" reprinted in *Women Unite!*, ed. Canadian Women's Educational Press (Toronto 1972), 53, 51

19. Mariarosa Dalla Costa and Selma James, *The Power of Women and the Subversion of the Community* (Bristol 1972).

20. Ann Oakley, *Subject Women* (New York 1981), 168

21. "The Housewife and Her Labour under Capitalism," *New Left Review* 83 (1974).

22. Jean Gardiner, "Women's Domestic Labour," *New Left Review* 89 (1975), 58

23. John Harrison, "The Political Economy of Housework," *Bulletin of the Conference of Socialist Economists* (Winter 1973), 43

24. Margaret Coulson, Bianka Magas and Hilary Wainwright, "The Housewife and Her Labour under Capitalism — A Critique," *New Left Review* 89 (1975).

25. Paul Smith, "Domestic Labour and Marx's Theory of Value," in *Feminism and Materialism,* ed. Annette Kuhn and Anne Marie Wolpe (London 1978).

26. Seccombe, "Domestic Labour", 9

27. Coulson, Magas and Wainwright, "The Housewife — A Critique," 49

28. Jean Gardiner, "Political Economy of Domestic Labour in Capitalist Society," in *Dependence and Exploitation in Work and Marriage,* ed. Diana Leonard Barker and Sheila Allen (London 1976).

29. Maxine Molyneux, "Beyond the Domestic Labour Debate," *New Left Review* 116 (1979), 9

30. Wally Seccombe, "Domestic Labour — A Reply to Critics," *New Left Review* 94 (1975), 89

31. Ibid., 92

32. Wally Seccombe, "The Expanded Reproduction Cycle of Labour Power in Twentieth-Century Capitalism," in Fox, *Hidden in the Household.* (See n.2 above.)

33. Patricia Connelly, "Women's Work and Family Wage in Canada," in *Women and the World of Work*, ed. Anne Hoiberg (New York 1982), 223-38

34. Seccombe, "Expanded Reproduction Cycle." (See n.32 above.)

35. Christine Delphy, "L'ennemi principal," reprinted in *Libération des femmes année zéro,* ed. Partisans (Paris 1972).

36. Roberta Hamilton, *The Liberation of Women* (London 1978).

37. Dorothy Smith, "Women, The Family and Corporate Capitalism," in *Women in Canada*, ed. Marylee Stephenson (Toronto 1973), 45

38. Bonnie Fox, "Women's Double Work Day: Twentieth-Century Changes in the Reproduction of Daily Life," in Fox, *Hidden in the Household.*

39. Jean Gardiner, "Women in the Labour Process and Class Structure," in *Class and Class Structure,* ed. Alan Hunt (London 1977), 158

40. Christine Delphy, "Women in Stratification Studies," in *Doing Feminist Research,* ed. Helen Roberts (London 1981), 115

41. Hamilton, *Liberation,* 81. (See n.36 above.)

42. Gayle Rubin, "The Traffic in Women: Notes on the Political Economy of Sex," in *Toward an Anthropology of Women,* ed. Rayna R. Reiter (New York 1975), 165

43. Richard W. Wertz and Dorothy C. Wertz, *Lying-In: A History of Childbirth in America* (New York 1979), ix

44. Louise A. Tilly and Joan W. Scott, *Women, Work and Family* (New York 1978), 27

45. Wertz and Wertz, *Lying-In,* 3. (See n.43 above.)

46. Margaret Llewelyn Davies, *Maternity: Letters from Working Women* (1915; Tiptree, Essex 1978), 6

47. Neil Sutherland, *Children in English-Canadian Society* (Toronto 1976), 62-3

48. Janice Delaney, Mary Jane Lupton and Emily Toth, *The Curse* (New York 1977), 42-3

49. Joyce Leeson and Judith Gray, *Women and Medicine* (London 1978), 93

50. Quoted in Sheila Rowbotham, *A New World for Women: Stella Browne — Socialist Feminist* (London 1977), 63, 62

51. Linda Gordon, "The Struggle for Reproductive Freedom: Three Stages of Feminism," in *Capitalist Patriarchy and the Case for Feminist Socialism,* ed. Zillah Eisenstein (New York 1979), 108

52. For accounts of the historical development of regulations related to abortion, see Angus McLaren, "Women's Work and the Regulation of Family Size: The Question of Abortion in the Nineteenth Century," *History Workshop* 4 (1977); and idem, "Birth Control and Abortion in Canada, 1870-1920," *Canadian Historical Review* 59: 3 (September 1978), 319-40

53. Wertz and Wertz, *Lying-In.*

54. *Women, Work and Family,* 100. (See n.44 above.)

55. "Women's Work," 76. (See n.52 above.)

56. Sutherland, *Children,* 56. (See n.47 above.)

57. Canada, Statistics Canada, *Canada Year Book 1975* (Ottawa 1975), 153

58. Leroy O. Stone and Claude Marceau, *Canadian Population Trends and Public Policy Through the 1980s.* (Montreal, 1977), 37

59. Adrienne Rich, *Of Woman Born* (London 1977).

60. Barbara Ehrenreich and Deirdre English, *Complaints and Disorders* (Old Westbury, New York 1973), 72

61. Quoted by McLaren, "Birth Control," 320. (See n.52 above.)

62. "Reproductive Freedom," xiii. (See n.51 above.)

63. "Women's Work," 79

64. McLaren, "Birth Control," 320

65. Suzann Buckley, "Ladies or Midwives? Efforts to Reduce Infant and Maternal Mortality," in *A Not Unreasonable Claim,* ed. Linda Kealey (Toronto 1979), 140

66. Ehrenreich and English, *Complaints and Disorders,* 16. (See n.60 above.)

67. Wertz and Wertz, *Lying-In.*

68. Rainer Baehre, "Victorian Psychiatry and Canadian Motherhood," *Canadian Women's Studies* 2:1 (1980), 45

69. Davies, *Maternity,* 3. (See n.46 above.)

70. For an outstanding example of the type of historical investigation we have in mind, see Patricia Connelly and Martha MacDonald, "Women's Work: Domestic and Wage Labour in a Nova Scotia Community," in this issue of *Studies in Political Economy.*

Angela Miles

Economism and Feminism: Hidden in the Household
A Comment on the Domestic Labour Debate

What has come to be called the domestic labour debate originated in Marxist critiques of the political analysis of housework that Selma James and Mariarosa Dalla Costa developed in the early 1970s.[1] James and Dalla Costa followed Italian social capital theory[2] in arguing that today the working class is no longer the nineteenth-century proletariat defined by Marx; it now encompasses white- as well as blue-collar workers, and the wageless as well as the waged worker. This theory holds: (1) that the massification of labour and the sheer volume of production in advanced capitalism is breaking down occupational divisions within the working class; (2) that the new level of productive forces in advanced capitalism has broken the traditional capitalist connection between hours of labour time and the amount of surplus value created; (3) that these developments, and the resulting massive increase in wealth, are opening the way for a qualitatively new level of workers' struggle built on the refusal of labour (and thus refusal of an alienated existence as labour power); and (4) that this struggle challenges the core of capitalist relations more directly and decisively than earlier forms of workers' struggle based on the right to work (and to exist as labour power).

Dalla Costa and James drew out the implications of this perspective, not just for the wageless male worker in developed industrial societies, but for the wageless in the home and in the Third World.[3] They argued that the best way to articulate the struggle against labour was for the wageless to demand wages. They developed their position most fully within the women's movement in respect to housewives, arguing that their demand for wages would aggravate the contradictions of a society that had outgrown the material base of capitalist social relations and social control organized around the wage.

The revision of Marx's analysis of the role of labour in the creation of surplus value in earlier capitalist economies throws into question the analytical and strategic importance of his distinction between productive and unproductive labour. It is this, and not a misunderstanding of these concepts or of the significance that Marx assigned to them, that underlies the willingness of Dalla Costa and James to argue that it is no longer *politically* relevant to distinguish housework from waged work on the grounds that it is "unproductive." In this they echo Marx's own critical method: the analysis of existing society entails an essential political moment and the necessary direction of liberatory struggle is contained/revealed in the social critique itself.

Neither of the two main Marxist responses to the "wages for housework" analysis has addressed the perspective at a theoretical/political level. One set of critical literature has focused on the immediate practical and tactical implications of the demand for wages for housework. It raises such questions as "Who will pay the wages?" and "Will payment for housework institutionalize this degrading labour?" But it does not recognize or refute the general analysis of late capitalism on the basis of which this strategic demand is posited.[4] The other main critique took issue, not with the general analysis of capitalism or the call for a struggle against labour, but with the claim of James and Dalla Costa that housework produces surplus value.[5] By focusing on this question without addressing the wider questions which underlie it, this critique tended to limit a potentially important political debate to questions of textual exegesis. It assessed the wages for housework analysis in relation to established Marxist categories rather than in relation to the world and the possibilities for liberatory struggle.

Marxist categories were not originally developed to deal with labour in the home. There is, in any case, room for debate about such conceptions as "productive labour" even in reference to the sphere of waged labour.[6] So it is not surprising that wide differences emerged even among those who agreed that this textual exercise was important. It is around these differences that the domestic labour debate has developed. The genesis of the debate thus lies in the reduction of such large theoretical and political questions as the nature of class in advanced capitalism, and the relationship of class and gender oppression to a narrow economic analysis of domestic labour under capitalism.

The book, *Hidden in the Household: Women's Domestic Labour Under Capitalism*, ably edited by Bonnie Fox, brings together many recent Canadian contributions to the domestic labour debate. Its recent appearance provides a good opportunity for me to substantiate my charge of this literature's economism and to examine the limitations inherent in it.[7]

In his two articles, Wally Seccombe critiques and extends Marxist categories in an attempt to develop a general analysis of the capitalist mode of production that can encompass areas of capitalist reality with which Marx and Marxists have not dealt. Bruce Curtis, Linda Briskin, Bonnie Fox, Emily Blumenfeld and Susan Mann take a less dynamic approach. They focus on more specific moments of that reproduction, and are more concerned to preserve than to develop Marxist categories. Nevertheless, they take widely different positions on such "classical" questions of the debate as whether this labour can or cannot be analyzed in terms of Marx's labour theory of value, whether it creates surplus value, and whether its privatization is necessary to capitalism.

Wally Seccombe's articles are a major development of his own earlier work and an original contribution to the debate. He distinguishes "four interrelated facets of the mode of production: (a) the mode of appropriation of the producers' product by the producers; (b) the mode of its distribution among producers; (c) the mode of its consumption in the domestic group; and (d) the mode of labour power's production, both on a daily and on a generational basis."[8] He then asks, "What becomes of the categories, 'forces' and 'relations' of production under the foregoing treatment of the mode of subsistence?" and answers: "In each case these categories must be stretched to incorporate the subsistence dimension. Productive forces must include both the technological means of production and the capacities of the producers."[9] The bulk of his two articles reflect his attempts to do this "stretching" and, in the process, to "salvage the essential categories of Marx's political economy from a reductionist tendency."[10]

Many of the other articles in the book express skepticism about whether this is salvage or sabotage. The domestic labour debate consists in large part of varying positions on this question of the admissibility of stretching Marx's categories and on the correct way to apply stretched or unstretched categories. The narrow economic and textual limits of these questions are not in themselves a significant political problem. However, these limits go unrecognized by most of the contributors to the domestic labour literature who tend to mistake their essentially economic analysis for political analysis. In the rest of this article I want to document the presumed identity between economic analysis and political theory in this literature and to outline its grave consequences for the development of radical theory and practice.

The most obvious instance of economist confusion is the general tendency to present an analysis of domestic labour as if it were a theoretical examination of the oppression of women. All the authors in *Hidden in the Household* write as if patriarchal power and gender domination were a central concern of their work: Bonnie Fox's introduction identifies "the issue of the relation between capitalism and patriarchy" as "crucial"[11] and calls the "structural determinants of women's oppression" a "key question."[12] Bruce Curtis's main aim is to rebut the argument "that the domestic sphere emerges as a plot on the part of male workers and capitalists to oppress women and children."[13] Linda Briskin investigates domestic labour in order to achieve a "better understanding of women's oppression (and to clarify) the strategic political questions facing the women's movement."[14] Emily Blumenfeld and Susan Mann claim to "illuminate the intersection of sexual oppression and class oppression."[15]

In fact the authors *describe* women's oppression. They do not *analyze* it. They all acknowledge, in varying degrees, the specific "dependence" and "oppression" of women under capitalism. Curtis says "her dependency and isolation separate her position from his."[16] Briskin describes oppression as opposed to exploitation, as a "condition that takes many forms, including racism and sexism."[17] Fox says that "within the working class, women have special interests. They occupy a unique position because of their sex. Domestic labourers are dependent on a *man's* wage (or on state subsidies)"[18] Seccombe develops a finely observed and original description of "the prerogatives that accrue to the primary breadwinner, by virtue of his personal appropriation of the bulk of the family's income."[19] These, he argues, form "a powerful basis for petty male dominance in the proletarian household."[20] But, with the exception of Curtis's article[21] these observations lead to no theoretical questions about *why* this might be and how one can explain the fact that capitalist relations (and not only capitalist relations) have developed in such a way as to ensure men's power over women.

The kinds of questions the domestic labour debate is built around do not address the causes or significance of women's oppression. Rather, they presume it and seek to understand the mechanisms of its institutionalization in capitalist society — a very different level of analysis that is reflected in the following sample questions from the book: "Is the socialization of domestic labour in fact possible under capitalism?" "Is the relationship between the household and capitalist production changing?"[22] "How does the law of value shape the reproduction cycle of labour power?"²³ "What is the effect on the socialization of domestic labour and the increased participation of women in the labour force? Under what conditions is domestic labour intensified? What is the effect of domestic technology and the expansion of consumer goods production on the household? What happens with large families, single workers? What influences the level of wages? What is the developmental dynamic of the 'family wage'? When does child care change in form? Under what impetus does the state socialize services or remove them? How do women participate in the class struggle? What is the role of the family in the class struggle?"²⁴

The authors all explicitly recognize that the analysis of capitalism as such can throw no light on the vexed question of why it is invariably women who do the labour in the home. Curtis notes that "while an examination of the structural features of capitalism reveals the structural bases of domestic labour and the working family, it does not explain the sex-based division of labour between working class men and women."²⁵ Blumenfeld and Mann note that the sexual division of labour is not theoretically necessary to capitalism: "Equally obvious (although of no necessity) is the fact that it is generally the woman who prepares the food and feeds the family within the context of the privatized household."²⁶ Briskin remarks that "The question why women traditionally do domestic labour requires a separate investigation."²⁷ Seccombe explains that the "unequal value (of men and women's) respective labour powers on the market . . . impresses an unequal division of labour on them,"²⁸ but this does not (and I doubt that he would claim that it does) explain that unequal value.

The failure to tackle qustions of gender domination at a theoretical level leaves these articles in the strange position of both acknowledging (descriptively) and denying (theoretically) women's oppression. Bonnie Fox notices that "domestic labourers are dependent on a *man's* wage" only to say, at the same time, that "the domestic labourer owns her own means of production."²⁹ Blumenthal and Mann deny the fact of men's power over women even as they recognize its results: "As the 'sanctity' of privacy allows the household to close its doors to public scrutiny and supervision it is not surprising that the household in modern society remains the major arena of personal violence: wife battering and child abuse are the very products of privatization."³⁰ Women's economic dependence goes a lot further to explain their vulnerability to these attacks than the privatization of the home. But women's economic position alone cannot account for the attacks. How is it that Blumenfeld and Mann feel no need to ask why "unsupervised" men routinely attack women and children in our culture? To ask this question breaches the economic limits of the domestic labour debate. But surely it is a question that must disturb those attempting to build a new and better world, and one that must have some place in our development of theory.

Wally Seccombe, in examining the "core condition of women's oppression under capitalism," is more careful than others in the book to avoid any suggestion that he is examining the causes of women's oppression in general. Nevertheless the schizophrenia involved in noticing that oppression, while at the same time avoiding the question of its causes and meaning, is more pronounced in his work because his descriptive treatment is fuller. He notices that "In the confines of (the) rationality (of the household budget) women's needs and interests are normally subordinated."[31] But he chooses not to examine the ways and degree to which men and women's interests differ individually and collectively, and whether that difference is reflected in the operation of the law of value. Instead he focuses, like the other authors in the book, on the shared interests of men and women in the household in "securing subsistence" within the constraints of the capitalist mode of production. He argues that taking "the family unit and not the individual wage labourer" as the starting point is "an exemplary methodologial premise for the contemporary study not only of women's labour but the whole question of the allocation of the working class's total labour time between the sexes and between the two production sites."[32] Clearly, however, taking the household as the basic analytical unit specifically precludes consideration of the allocation of total labour time *between* the sexes. It means necessarily presenting such questions as whether to "intensify domestic labour, shift its focus or seek a second wage"[33] as if the optimum choice were the same for the man and woman. In describing the tensions involved in the "household" attempts to maximize the standard of living and minimize the labour effort, he writes as if there were only one standard of living and labour effort in a household. In fact there are two and the trade-offs between them are direct. Less leisure for the woman means more for the man.[34] More important, the trade-offs involve, not only material goods and physical effort, but power as well. A paid job for the woman may bring more money into the household but threaten the man's power. The documentation of actual working-class family interaction in such books as *Coal Is Our Life* by Fernando Henriques, and *Worlds of Pain* by Lillian Breslow Ruben shows clearly that power considerations such as these play a big part in "household" decisions.

The unequal value of male and female labour on the market makes it "rational" in household economic terms for the woman to stay at home if one of the adults must do so. But it cannot account for the fact that it is the woman who is responsible for domestic labour even when she is in the paid labour force. It is clearly not in her interest that this should be so. Although the greater economic power of the male might explain his ability to impose this situation, it does not explain why he does so.

If it is true that even the most original and far-reaching of contributions to the domestic labour debate throws no theoretical light on the substance and causes of gender domination, how can all these authors make this claim for their work? Their claim rests on the mistaken belief that to show the significance of capitalism in shaping women's oppression is to adequately explain this oppression in class terms.

These articles all demonstrate the unexceptionable, even obvious (though partial), truth that women's responsibility for domestic labour performed in the privatized household is the specific form in which women's oppression is institutionalized under capitalism. But to document this is not to deal with the question of *why* capitalist relations have developed in such a way as to ensure women's subordination to men. To illustrate that women's oppression takes specific forms under capitalism is *not* to prove that it is derivative. The authors' belief that it is leads them to pose a false dichotomy between gender and class domination. Therefore they read any serious theoretical attention to gender oppression as a domination that is not, or may not be, derivative of class, as a denial of the influence and even the existence of class exploitation.

Over and over again the authors describe feminist attempts to understand the universality of gender oppression as if such attempts necessarily involve a denial of its historical and cultural specificity in different times and places, and specifically under capitalism: "Those attempts at an analysis of women's oppression that begin with the assumption of women's universal subordination are inherently limited. In ignoring the marked historical and cross-cultural variations in women's position, these analyses abandon the search for causally related material and social factors before it has really begun."[35]

The attempts of feminist radicals of all stripes (Marxist, socialist, radical and lesbian) to move toward a new, more universal analysis of domination that can encompass both class and gender oppression[36] are presented as a simple substitution of gender for class: "This analysis presents capitalists and male workers as sharing a common interest in the oppression of women. The exploitation of labour power by capital, which itself structures the oppression of working class women, is *replaced* by a conception in which men in general oppress women in general."[37]

The reductionist presumption that one must deal theoretically *either* with class *or* gender domination limits the development of dialogue around the question of the relationship and genesis of the two. We have seen how in this volume it leads to the mistaken belief that studies of the shape of women's oppression under capitalism are analyses of its causes. It also reduces all feminism to reformism and renders invisible the attempts of feminist radicalism to tackle both class and gender domination.

Emily Blumenfeld and Susan Mann make this reduction explicitly when they move from the fact that feminists "maintain that the oppression of women is the most fundamental and deep-rooted form of oppression, and that the struggle for sexual liberation must not be subordinated to any other" to the presumption that this means that for feminists "the transcendence of women's oppression (is) separate from the question of the abolition of private property" and "sexual oppression and class oppression (are) two distinct issues."[38] There are reformist feminists who seek women's equality within capitalism. But the hallmark of feminist radicalism is a commitment to explore what we believe are the deep and common roots of *all* forms of oppression. This becomes essential when the defining value of the struggle is the end of domination and alienation rather than the end of private property and the equality of material distribution. It is not to ignore the specificity of the changing shape of different dominations or their relationship, but to develop, through an analysis of their specificity, an understanding that can guide our struggle for the freedom of all.

Many of us have come to this through Marxism. Whether we call ourselves Marxist, socialist, radical or lesbian feminists, our heritage from that tradition is to demand of ourselves a theoretical understanding of the totality of our society that goes beyond appearances. We retain a commitment to a dialectical, historical and materialist methodology. In fact, the complexity of a project that seeks to understand both patriarchal and class power has meant that we cannot so easily slip into the economist reductionism that bedevils Marxism and that is evident in the domestic labour debate's presumption to explain women's oppression.

The psychological and economic, personal and political, individual and social components of life and analysis have to be brought together to begin to tackle the questions feminists raise. How is it, for instance, that the abolition of private property fails to secure women's freedom and, indeed, worker's freedom? Marxism has shown that the existence of relative surplus is a necessary precondition to the emergence of private property in goods and the means of production (though not, apparently in women) and to class power based on it. Relative surplus however, is surely not a sufficient condition. It does not, alone, explain why men's (the term is used advisedly here) response to surplus was private appropriation.

Feminism, dealing as it does with oppression by fathers of sons and daughters, husbands of wives, and lovers of "loved" ones, is forced to face such difficult questions. And they arise, too, around the origins of class in ways they have not yet done within Marxism.

Feminists would want to ask of this volume such questions as: How is it that self-interest is often experienced by men, even in personal life and even in the common struggle of working class households for subsistence, in terms of individual and collective *male* power and advantage? Can this really be explained as a survival requirement of the capitalist mode of production;[39] a result of the unequal law of value for male and female labour;[40] the product of the privatization of the household;[41] or pollution by "the patriarchal institutions and practices of the ruling class and state"?[42]

Is an analysis of the capitalist family "as an integral part of the capitalist reality" sufficient to end the "mystification of the relations in the home" in which the "locus of tension becomes the relation between the domestic labourer and the wage labourer?"[43]

Can the relations between men and women, and men's oppression of women — even in their capitalist forms — be encompassed by the respective terms "wage labourer" and "domestic labourer"? How can one deal in this framework with such systematic male violence against women as rape, prostitution (including child prostitution and the large international trade in women), pornography, incest, wife beating and sexual harassment (to leave aside such non-capitalist practices as sutti, witch burning, clitorectomy and foot binding)?

Is the feminist contention that male workers as well as male capitalists protect patriarchal power adequately refuted by showing, as Curtis does, that the "domestic sphere (did not emerge) as a plot on the part of male workers and capitalists to oppress women and children"? Is it true that the working class "struggle to limit the working day became a struggle to limit the participation of women and children in industrial labour" because the working class was "forced to fight the battle" on the sexist grounds established by the English bourgeoisie's exclusion of women from the "rights of freeborn Englishmen . . . to sell their labour as they saw fit"?[44] Did the working class use bourgeois sexism to gain a point? Or did the bourgeoisie use working class sexism to limit the struggle? Was it a bit of both and might this help explain the persistence of patriarchal power without a cross-class conspiracy thesis?

Can the political case for an autonomous women's movement be made adequately without reference to the power and interest differences between men and women, on the purely economic grounds that "women's oppression is rooted in the capitalist family, which exists outside the sphere of commodity production"?[45]

The presumption that these kinds of questions can only arise from a position that denies or trivializes class exploitation is the basis of traditional Marxists' confusion of feminist radicalism with feminist reformism, and their dismissal of both as "bourgeois feminism." The political costs of this are high because it insulates Marxist theory and practice from the creative challenge of recent work by feminists. It has meant that the theoretical debate around class and gender is developing within feminist radicalism rather than also within Marxism.

The domestic labour debate, focused as it is on women's work, with its claims to analyse women's oppression, is well placed to acknowledge these questions and to open the dialogue between feminists and Marxists. Unfortunately, the false identity posed between women's oppression and domestic labour under capitalism leads to an acceptance of, rather than a challenge to, Marxist definitions which render feminist *radicalism* invisible and exclude its questions from Marxist dialogue.

This explains how it is that all but one of the authors in this volume can claim to deal theoretically with patriarchy and class without referring to the existing, well-developed feminist literature on the question. Seccombe, who is least guilty of claims to be analyzing women's oppression in general, cites recent feminist historical, anthropological and philosophical work. Curtis joins him in referring to the recent Marxist-feminist collection of writings in political economy, *Feminism and Materialism: Women and Modes of Production*, edited by Annette Kuhn and Ann Marie Wolpe. Apart from this, reference to socialist and Marxist-feminist analysis is restricted to extremely early work: Margaret Benston's *The Political Economy of Women's Liberation* (1969); Maria Rosa Dalla Costa's *Women, Subversion and the Community* (1972) and Sheila Rowbotham's *Women's Consciousness, Man's World* (1973). The *only* radical feminist work cited is Shulamith Firestone's *Dialectic of Sex* (1970). Even the classical article, "Housework: Slavery or Labour of Love" (1970), in which the radical feminist, Betsy Warrior, developed the first analysis of domestic labour as producer of the commodity labour power, is overlooked.[46]

All the early articles cited are seminal works and deserve attention. But ten further years of theoretical writing in anthropology, history, psychology, sociology, philosophy as well as political economy have passed unacknowledged. There is no requirement for analysts of domestic labour to cite this literature, but when they claim to analyze gender oppression, its absence becomes a grave weakness. The weakness is especially evident in the Curtis and Blumenfeld and Mann articles which attempt a direct critique of feminist theory.

Many people, among them, I am sure, some of the contributors to this volume, would argue that any Marxist analysis must aim to be historical, dialectical and material and to bring together the political and the economic. This may, in fact, explain the persistent, unfounded claims to do this, made in the domestic labour debate by its participants. My purpose here, however, has not been to argue that writing on domestic labour *must* deal with the theoretical questions raised by the oppression of women and feminist analysis of that oppression. It is not the debate's economic analysis of domestic labour, but the fact that it presents the analysis as a theoretical treatment of gender and class, that dooms it to economism. Therefore, I would urge one of two courses on those working in the area: *either* they should develop a definition of their project which recognizes more realistically limited economic parameters and breaks with the claim to encompass the gender/class debate, *or* they should open the debate beyond its economic limits by defining parameters in ways that recognize the questions that feminists are raising. The debate would then move beyond itself to the extent that it could no longer be called "the domestic labour debate." It would be a major contribution to the initiation of an already too long delayed Marxist/feminist dialogue.

Notes

1. See: Mariarosa Dalla Costa, *The Power of Women and the Subversion of the Community*, (Bristol 1972); Selma James, *Women, the Unions and Work*.

2. For an introduction to this theory in English see Guido Baldi, "Thesis on Mass Worker and Social Capital," *Radical America* 6:3 (1973), 3-21.

3. See Selma James, "Sex, Race and Working Class Power," *Race Today* (January 1974), 12-15

4. For examples of this literature see Sheila Rowbotham, "The Carrot, the Stick and the Movement," Caroline Freeman, "When is a Wage Not a Wage?" and Joan Landes, "Wages for Housework: Political and Theoretical Considerations," all anthologized in *The Politics of Housework*, ed. Ellen Malos (London 1980). See also Linda Briskin, "Toward Socialist Feminism? The Women's Movement: Where is it Going?" *Our Generation* 10:3 (1974), 23-34

5. Wally Seccombe's article, "The Housewife and Her Labour Under Capitalism," *New Left Review* 83 (1974), is an important example of this approach. Other examples are "The Housewife and Her Labour Under Capitalism — A Critique," by Margaret Carlson, Branka Magas and Hilary Wainwright; "Women's Domestic Labour" by Jean Gardiner, Susan Himmelweit and Maureen Mackintosh (also anthologized in E. Malos, ed., *The Politics of Housework*. (See n. 4 above.)

6. See Ian Gough, "Marx's Theory of Productive and Unproductive Labour," *New Left Review* 76 (1972).

7. Bonnie Fox, ed., *Hidden in the Household: Women's Domestic Labour Under Capitalism* (Toronto 1980).

8. Wally Seccombe, "Domestic Labour and the Working Class Household," in Fox, *Hidden in the Household*, 31. (See n. 7 above.)

9. Ibid., 33

10. Ibid., 27

11. Bonnie Fox, "Introduction," in Fox, *Hidden in the Household*, 15

12. Ibid., 21

13. Bruce Curtis, "Capital, The State and the Origins of the Working Class Household," in Fox, *Hidden in the Household*, 121

14. Linda Briskin, "Domestic Labour: A Methodological Discussion," in Fox, *Hidden in the Household*, 136

15. Emily Blumenfeld and Susan Mann, "Domestic Labour and the Reproduction of Labour Power: Towards an Analysis of Women, the Family, and Class," in Fox, *Hidden in the Household*, 267

16. Curtis, "Capital," 109. (See n. 13 above.)

17. Briskin, "Domestic Labour," 137. (See n. 14 above.)

18. Bonnie Fox, "Women's Double Work Day: Twentieth-Century Changes in the Reproduction of Daily Life," in Fox, *Hidden in the Household* (See n. 7 above.)

19. Seccombe, "Domestic Labour," 83. (See n. 8 above.)

20. Ibid., 84

21. Bruce Curtis's article is the only one in this volume to focus theoretically on the question of women's oppression. In doing so it falls outside the limits of the domestic labour debate strictly defined. It is not by chance that his is also the only article to engage the wages for housework perspective directly.

22. Fox, 13, 14-15

23. Seccombe, "The Expanded Reproduction Cycle of Labour Power in Twentieth Century Capitalism," in Fox, *Hidden in the Household*, 217

24. Briskin, "Domestic Labour," 169

25. Curtis, "Capital," 130

26. Blumenfeld and Mann, "Domestic Labour," 293

27. Briskin, "Domestic Labour," 143

28. Seccombe, "Expanded Reproduction," 228

29. Fox, "Women's Double Work Day," 190. (See n. 18 above.)

30. Blumenfeld and Mann, "Domestic Labour," 273

31. Seccombe, "Expanded Reproduction," 228

32. Ibid., 239

33. Ibid., 222

34. For an examination of differential material conditions for men and women in marriage, see Laura Oren, "The Welfare of Women in Labouring Families: England, 1860-1950," in *Feminist Studies* 1: 3-4 (1973), 107-125.

35. Bonnie Fox, "Introduction," 11/12. Similar assertions include: "The argument concerning the enduring nature of patriarchy from precapitalist to fully capitalist societies often obscures, however, the revolution which has occurred *in the way* in which patriarchal domination is sustained within the household of the working class' (Seccombe, "Domestic Labour," 81); "Once the historical nature of the family is established, the theory of a continuous system of patriarchy, identified with the family is called into question." (Briskin, "Domestic Labour," 147).

36. For references to the socialist feminist literature of this project and a feminist examination and critique of the progress made so far, see Iris Young, "Socialist Feminism and the Limitations of Dual Systems Theory," *Socialist Review* 50-51 (1980), 169-188.

37. Curtis, "Capital," 121

38. Blumenfeld and Mann, "Domestic Labour," 268, 268, 269

39. Briskin, "Domestic Labour," 153

40. Seccombe, "Expanded Reproduction," 273

41. Blumenfeld and Mann, "Domestic Labour," 273

42. Seccombe, "Domestic Labour," 86

43. Briskin, "Domestic Labour," 146

44. Curtis, "Capital," 121, 126

45. Briskin, "Domestic Labour," 138

46. This article is reprinted in *Radical Feminism*, ed. Anne Loedt (New York 1973).

Patricia Connelly

On Marxism and Feminism

Recently the issue of class and gender has been raised in the pages of *Studies in Political Economy* — by Angela Miles in "Economism and Feminism; *Hidden in the Household*: A Comment on the Domestic Labour Debate,"[1] and by Pat Armstrong and Hugh Armstrong in "Beyond Sexless Class and Classless Sex: Towards Feminist Marxism."[2] These authors argue that we need more dialogue around this issue to develop a framework appropriate for the explanation of women's oppression under capitalism. In the spirit of such a dialogue, I would like to comment on several of their points. In addition, I will draw on some arguments made by Michelle Barrett in *Women's Oppression Today: Problems in Marxist Feminist Analysis*.[3]

In her review of Canadian contributions to the domestic labour debate, Angela Miles argues that the authors claim to be providing a theoretical analysis of gender and class but that the questions posed and the concepts used in the debate do not address the causes or significance of women's oppression. Moreover, radical feminist attempts to "move towards a new more universal analysis of domination that can encompass both class and gender oppression" are presented by the authors as a substitution of gender for class and then dismissed. She concludes that since the debate ignores feminist questions and thus reduces women's oppression to a narrow economic focus, even the most original and far-reaching contribution has no theoretical insight into the substance and origins of gender domination. Moreover, their claim to do so stands in the way of initiating an "already too long delayed Marxist/feminist dialogue."

It is true, as Miles points out, that the contributors to *Hidden in the Household* do not explain the causes of women's oppression, but in her review she reproduces quotes which clearly state that they are not trying to explain the historical causes of gender inequality; they are trying rather to reveal the structural basis of domestic labour and by so doing uncover some mechanisms by which women have been subordinated under capitalism. With regard to the issue of patriarchy, some of the authors may have overstated their case, but my sense is that their discussion was not meant as a dismissal of gender relations but rather as a reference to the fact that in general, radical feminist analyses have given primacy to patriarchy over the capitalist mode of production. Earlier feminist works such as those by Kate Millet and by Shulamith Firestone, for example, use patriarchy to mean a universal trans-historical category of male dominance grounded in the logic of biological reproduction, while more recent feminist works such as Christine Delphy's use patriarchy to focus on social rather than biological relations. Delphy argues that since men appropriate the unpaid labour of women through the institution of marriage, the material oppression of women lies in patriarchal relations of production within the family. Although the emphasis is different, these authors all give patriarchy analytic independence and analytic primacy over the capitalist mode of production.[4]

In a short review essay, Angela Miles cannot be expected to have presented fully her own position on this issue. She alludes to it, however, when discussing what she considers the basis for a Marxist and feminist dialogue. She says that "the defining value of the struggle is the end of domination and alienation rather than the end of private property and equality of material distribution."[5] There is no doubt that she means class as well as gender domination, but if the struggle is defined in terms of domination in general rather than class or property relations, it seems fair to ask what would then be the central contradiction — the basis for social change — in capitalist society?

While these first points raised by Miles refer specifically to the contributions in *Hidden in the Household*, her conclusions refer more generally to the entire domestic labour debate. In general, it is true to say that the domestic labour debate has focused narrowly on structural categories and has not addressed the totality of women's oppression. It is not true, however, to say that the domestic labour debate has made no theoretical contribution to an understanding of the significance of this oppression. Nor is it correct to say that the domestic labour debate has stood in the way of initiating a dialogue over gender and class. Indeed, I would argue that the domestic labour debate has advanced our understanding by demonstrating that women's oppression has a material basis and is linked to the political economy of capitalist society through their domestic and wage labour. It has also contributed to the debate that is well underway between Marxists and feminists and among Marxist feminists in such works as Eisenstein's *Capitalist Patriarchy and the Case for Socialist Feminism*; Kuhn and Wolpe's *Feminism and Materialism*; Sargent's *The Unhappy Marriage of Marxism and Feminism*; Barrett's *Women's Oppression Today*; and closer to home, in the pages of *Atlantis*.[5]

Within this dialogue the issue has emerged as follows: in very general and simplistic terms, Marxist analysis focuses on the relations of production without distinguishing between women's and men's experiences under capitalism. Radical feminist analysis focuses on the relations of gender without considering the specific historical and economic context of these relations. Marxist feminists are trying to develop an analysis of how unequal gender relations which preceded capitalism have been affected historically by capitalist relations of production — by class domination and class struggle. As the attempt to integrate both class and gender progresses, we find Marxists adding on women and radical feminists adding on class. The question is: how do we develop a coherent and integrated perspective with which to analyze the oppression of women in capitalist society?

This is the question addressed by Pat and Hugh Armstrong and by Michelle Barrett. While these authors agree on many points, they begin from different theoretical positions. The Armstrongs begin by providing an excellent summary and evaluation of the domestic labour debate, which lays the basis for their own analysis in which they "suggest ways to go forward in developing a political economy that comprehends the fundamental importance of sex divisions at all levels of analysis." They go on to develop their argument that the subordination of women is inherent in the capitalist mode of production. They say that "the sexual division of labour is essential to this mode of production, at the highest level of abstraction." The implication of this argument seems to be that if the inequality of women had not already existed, capitalism would have had to create it. The reason is that capitalism is premised on free wage labour. The reproduction of wage labour must take place in some kind of unit outside of the sphere of production of goods and services. Since women have babies, the separation of home and workplace seems "to imply a segregation, and denigration, of women." Indeed, they argue that the separation of home and workplace not only implies the segregation of women; it requires it. Thus "the existence of a sexual division of labour, although not its form or extent, is crucial to capitalism and therefore to its theorization." It is significant that they do not distinguish between "sex" and "gender," that is, the biologically determined and the socially assigned. Their position is that since these factors are interdependent and since sexual division of labour is the term most often used, no purpose is serviced by distinguishing analytically between them.

Michelle Barrett, on the other hand, uses the term gender and argues that gender divisions are not a necessary element of the capitalist mode of production. For Barrett the question of class is put in terms of the mode of production, while the question of gender is put in terms of the historical development of the social formation. Gender divisions preceded the capitalist mode of production. As capitalism developed, however, it adapted and used this existing division between men and women. Once this had occurred, women's subordination became entrenched in the capitalist system to the point where it became crucial. Nevertheless, gender divisions are an historically constituted integral part of, but not a necessary condition for, the capitalist mode of production.

According to Barrett, to go from the principle that capitalism requires the separation of home and workplace to the position that this separation requires the relegation of women to the home and their exclusion from wage labour is, in fact, precisely to accept the biologistic assumption that this outcome was inevitable. A more historical approach, says Barrett in referring to England, shows that the relegation of women to the home and to low-paid, segregated wage labour was a long and uneven process which involved a struggle between women and the better-organized male craft unionists. The questions of who would be responsible for childcare and whose skills would be recognized as more valuable in the workplace were resolved in the interest of men according to a division of labour and an ideology of gender which predated capitalism and which served to disadvantage women in their struggle. Barrett concludes that women's oppression in capitalist society is characterized by a particular form of family household that has both an ideological and material basis and that has a profound effect on the relationship between women's wage and domestic labour. It is important to point out that Armstrong and Armstrong agree with this conclusion since they argue that the sexual division of labour must be understood at all levels of analysis. The main difference then between the two positions revolves around whether or not the sexual or gendered division of labour is essential at the level of the capitalist mode of production. Let us consider in more detail the distinction that is being drawn.

The capitalist system can be analyzed at different levels of its organization. We can analyze it at the most abstract level to determine the structural boundaries of the system and how the economy in its purest form is structured, how it operates, and how it changes. Analysis at this level separates out what is absolutely essential to an understanding of the mechanics of the capitalist system. The focus is on the forces of production and the relations of production. The forces of production are continually developing and societal change occurs as the forces of production and the corresponding relations of production come into contradiction. This key contradiction takes the form of class struggle between those who are the producers and those who benefit from this production. It is through conflict and struggle between these two classes that change comes about. At this level of abstraction the aim is to uncover the underlying economic structures, that is, the logic which governs the operations of a capitalist system. In *Hidden in the Household*, Wally Seccombe makes a strong case for expanding the concept of the capitalist mode of production to include not only the production unit but also the subsistence unit. The subsistence sphere is, however, "structurally subordinate to the sphere of industrial production where capital presides directly over labour."[6] With this conception he argues that the household and domestic labour are a necessary part of the capitalist mode of production. However, for an explanation of the particular form of patriarchal family relations which exists in capitalist societies — that is, the prevalence of the nuclear family form, the ownership of household property overwhelmingly by men, the performance of domestic labour overwhelmingly by women — it is necessary to move from "the sexless and epochal abstraction of the capitalist mode of production" to the "sexist and historically periodized concrete of the developed capitalist societies."[7] This points to the fact that the general characteristics defined by the capitalist mode of production become specified by the historical circumstances of particular societies.

This brings us to another level of analysis, that is, to the more concrete and historically specific level of the capitalist social formation. This social formation contains several modes of production but is dominated by the capitalist mode of production with its fundamental labour/capital contradiction. The social formation contains groupings that derive from relations of production (e.g., classes) and groupings whose structures are determined by principles other than those of the relations of production (e.g., gender). It is within the social formation that struggle takes place. The point of this approach is not to reduce every relationship to economic terms (as at the level of the capitalist mode of production) but rather to disclose the relationship between the economic structure and these other structures (at the more concrete and empirical level of the social formation). An analysis at this level examines how the capitalist mode of production, as it operates in specific societies, determines or redefines particular social, political and ideological forms. At this level the focus is on how the relations of production intersect, combine and conflict with the relations of gender in different classes and in different historical periods within one society, and in different societies. The analysis also raises the question as to how class and gender structures combine, intersect and conflict in social formations dominated by other modes of production.

To use a different example, the reserve army of labour is both a necessary product of the capitalist accumulation process and it is a necessary condition for accumulation to occur. Therefore, a reserve army is essential to the capitalist mode of production. Some group must act as a reserve labour force. It is not, however, essential that this group be composed of women. It is only when we expand the concept of the reserve army and move from the abstract to the more concrete level that we can account for the historical and empirical reality of married women (or different groups of men for that matter) acting as a reserve army in Canada. At different points in history women, despite their chidbearing activities, have been brought into capitalist production, and at other points, when they were no longer needed, have been moved out. In recent years, as a result of changes in the economy and in the household, women have been drawn into the labour force on a relatively permanent part-time or full-time basis.[8] To analyze women's position at the level of the social formation in this way is not to relegate women to a secondary position or less important level of analysis. Rather it is a way of using the concepts developed by Marx to explain the operation of the capitalist system, in order to understand specific aspects of women's experience in a capitalist society.

At the same time there are aspects of women's oppression that cannot be understood in terms of these categories, and we should not try to squeeze women's reality into them.[9] We do need to develop new concepts as Angela Miles suggests and we also need to retain the analytic primacy of the mode of production as Armstrong and Armstrong, and Barrett, suggest. The analysis itself, however, should proceed at the level of the historical development of a specific social formation.

At this point it might be asked whether it really matters how or at what level the question is posed, since the reality of the gender division of labour, and of women's oppression as it is experienced, is the same either way. It matters because several theoretical and political implications follow from this distinction. First, since gender divisions preceded capitalism we cannot expect them to disappear necessarily or automatically with the demise of the capitalist mode of production. This has obvious implications for the women's movement. Second, this distinction allows us to reject assumptions about the functional necessity of women's work in favour of examining under historically specific conditions the role of female domestic and wage labour and its advantages and disadvantages for capital and/or the family household and/or women.[10] Third, this distinction allows us to focus more clearly on particular issues such as the fact that class struggle and women's struggle do not always coincide and that working-class and middle-class women do not always share the same forms of oppression. The struggle for the male family wage, for example, can both be in the interest of the working-class family-household and not in the long term interest of working-class women.[11] Fourth, it moves us away from the view that women's biology necessarily relegates them to a subordinate position. It is clearly true that women not men bear children, but the responsibility connected to, and the definition of, child rearing are socially not "naturally" determined. Political issues like the demand for maternity and paternity leave are based on the assumptions that the biological reality of child bearing should be taken into account but that women need not be entirely responsible for child rearing. Fifth, this distinction keeps us alert to the fact that capitalist penetration of developing countries affects women and the family household quite differently than did capitalist development in Canada. For example, the new international division of labour has created a new female proletariat in the Third World whose cheap labour power is drawn upon while their husbands remain unemployed.[12] And finally, this distinction directs our focus to an ideology of gender that has been incorporated into the dominant ideology. This in turn raises the issue of the construction of femininity and masculinity, laying the basis for a Marxist-feminist analysis of specifically feminist questions.

Notes

1. Angela Miles, "Economism and Feminism; *Hidden in the Household*: A Comment on the Domestic Labour Debate," *Studies in Political Economy* 11 (summer, 1983).

2. Pat Armstrong and Hugh Armstrong, "Beyond Sexless Class and Classless Sex: Towards Feminist Marxism," *Studies in Political Economy* 10 (winter 1983).

3. Michelle Barrett, *Women's Oppression Today: Problems in Marxist Feminist Analysis* (London 1980).

4. For an excellent discussion of the different uses of the concept of patriarchy, see Barrett, *Women's Oppression Today*.

5. Z. Eisenstein, ed., *Capitalist Patriarchy and the Case for Socialist Feminism* (New York 1979); A. Kuhn and A. Wolpe, eds., *Feminism and Materialism* (London 1978); L. Sargent, ed., *The Unhappy Marriage of Marxism and Feminism* (London 1981); R. Hamilton, "Working at Home," *Atlantis* 7:1 (1981); B. Curtis, "Rejecting Working at Home," *Atlantis* 8:1 (1982); R. Hamilton, "Reply to Curtis," *Atlantis* 8:1 (1982).

6. Wally Seccombe, "Domestic Labour and the Working-Class Household," in *Hidden in the Household: Women's Domestic Labour Under Capitalism*, ed. Bonnie Fox (Toronto 1980), 37

7. Ibid., 59

8. M.P. Connelly, *Last Hired, First Fired: Women in the Canadian Workforce* (Toronto 1978); Bonnie Fox, "Women's Double Work Day: Twentieth Century Changes in the Reproduction of Daily Life" in Fox, *Hidden in the Household* (see n. 6 above).

9. Hamilton, "Working at Home." (See n. 5 above.)

10. For a discussion of this point and point three below, see M.P. Connelly, "Women's Work, the Family Household and the Canadian Economy" (Paper delivered at the Canadian Sociology and Anthropology Association Meetings, Learned Societies, Vancouver, 1983).

11. M. Barrett and M. McIntosh, "The 'Family Wage': Some Problems for Socialists and Feminists," *Capital and Class* 11 (1980); J. Humphries, "The Working Class Family, Women's Liberation and Class Struggle:

The Case of Nineteenth Century British History," *Review of Radical Political Economics* 9:3 (1981).

12. H. Safa, "Runaway Shops and Female Employment: The Search for Cheap Labor," *Signs* 7:2 (1981).

Pat Armstrong and Hugh Armstrong

More on Marxism and Feminism
A Response to Patricia Connelly

Building on the work of Michèle Barrett, Patricia Connelly has in *SPE* 12 performed the useful service of clarifying some important differences between her position on women's oppression under capitalism, and our position, as set out in *SPE* 10.[1] While there is much with which we can agree in Connelly's comment, it would in our view also be useful to address some issues of continuing disagreement.

Part of our argument was that free-wage labour is a defining characteristic of capitalism, a characteristic that entails the reproduction of free-wage labourers to a certain extent *outside* the capitalist production process proper. In other words, free-wage labour entails the separation of a public, commodity-production unit from a private, subsistence unit. Given this separation, and given that women, not men, have the babies and can nurse them, mothers are, for a limited time at least, less able than men to participate fully in the labour force. Specifically, under the capitalist mode of production, in which commodities are valued to the point of being fetishized and the work performed to produce non-commodities is devalued, this separation provides a material basis for inequality between the sexes. Because it is the capitalist mode of production, and not biology *per se*, that renders women subordinate, their subordination must be considered when examining capitalism at all levels of abstraction.

For Connelly, by contrast, while women's subordination has become entrenched in the capitalist system to the extent that it has become "crucial," it has not become a "necessary condition" for the capitalist mode of production. Rather than being "essential" to this mode, at the highest level of abstraction, it is the historical result of unequal struggles of women and men in concrete social formations. Following Barrett, she argues that to infer from the separation of production and subsistence units, "the relegation of women to the home and their exclusion from wage labour is, in fact, precisely to accept the biologistic assumption that this outcome was inevitable."[2] Instead, an ideology of gender that predated capitalism was adapted in concrete historical circumstances by coalitions of the capitalist class and working-class men — especially in male craft unions — to construct a family-household system. This system laid the basis for the relegation of women to the home, for a sex-segregated labour force, and for the mutual reinforcement of these two developments.

We will not stress here our many points of agreement with Connelly and Barrett. Several, such as the observation that the sexual division of labour predated capitalism, and the emphasis on struggle and contradiction in shaping historically the content of sex differences under capitalism, were raised in our initial article.[3] Instead, we will indicate some of the difficulties we have with Barrett's important book and then take up the question posed by Connelly of the theoretical and political implications of our different positions.

One must start with a degree of scepticism regarding an argument that women's subordination should be explained exclusively in terms of historical developments in concrete, capitalist social formations when this subordination is to be found in each and every one of them. In the specific English and American cases examined by Barrett, our scepticism is deepened by her degree of reliance on the exclusivism practiced by male craft unions and on the "protective" legislation promoted by them as a causal factor. As Joanna Brenner and Maria Ramas have recently shown, these unions could not have had such a decisive impact on sex segregation in the English and American capitalist labour forces, given when the legislation was introduced, how few men were in these unions, the unions' ambivalent stances on women working for pay, and the inability of the unions to impose their wills on this and on other issues.[4] Barrett offers no explanation of why working-class men enjoyed the success she attributes to them here when they were so clearly unsuccessful elsewhere.

We also have more fundamental, theoretical difficulties with Barrett's analysis. She argues, correctly in our view, against dual-systems approaches that posit the independent existence of captialist and patriarchal structures and that limit Marxist analysis to the former. What is needed is a theory that links the different structures — the different kinds of inequality. Yet in the end, she herself seems to depend on a dual-systems approach, as Connelly suggests when she writes that "for Barrett the question of class is put in terms of the mode of production, while the question of gender is put in terms of the historical development of the social formation."[5] On the one hand: a sex-blind capitalism; on the other: a seemingly autonomous ideology of gender. But what is the material basis of this ideology? How has it had so profound an impact (or rather, set of impacts) in the several social formations? What are we to make of the distinction between the subordination of women having become so crucial to the capitalist mode of production and its not being essential to it?

The answer provided by Barrett, which we find unsatisfactory, is that the ideology is a pre-capitalist vestige taken over and shaped as capitalism developed historically in various social formations. Further explanation apparently awaits further historical study. Yet in the meantime we are left wondering why this vestige was shaped so consistently in this way (sex segregation in the labour force and female responsibility for most domestic labour as mutually reinforcing tendencies that promote the subordination of women) and when, if ever, a more general explanation will emerge. Will it only occur when, in positivistic fashion, enough bits of historical evidence have been accumulated? Or is it for Barrett impossible, in principle, to arrive at such a general explanation?

However, while we are wondering there are, as Connelly correctly points out, significant theoretical and political implications attached to the different positions (those of Connelly/Barrett and of ourselves). The first implication discussed by Connelly is that because gender divisions preceded capitalism there is no guarantee that they will automatically disappear with its demise. We agree wholeheartedly, but think our approach offers more than historical precedence on the question. Feminism cannot be collapsed simply into socialism, because with socialism comes the replacement of commodity/market forces with explicitly political forces — with the creation of the conditions for the full flowering of conscious human agency. This, after all, is a large part of socialism's appeal. In such a context, domestic labour will not be devalued by commodity fetishism, but *can* nevertheless be devalued — and women can be subordinated — under socialism unless feminists are vigorous participants in the ongoing struggle to define and achieve the socialist project, and unless socialist women and men are prepared to take their biological differences into account.

Second, Connelly warns against yielding to assumptions of functional necessity — assumptions that have often plagued contributions to the domestic labour debate. We think our approach, with its emphasis on a method that is historical and dialectical as well as materialist, and with its focus on struggle and contradiction, avoids such assumptions while also avoiding both the restriction of attention to historically specific conditions — in particular, social formations and theoretically unspecified arguments about what is "crucial" to capitalism.

Third, she points out that class struggle and women's struggle (as "class" is now perceived) do not always coincide, and that working-class and middle-class women do not always share the same form of oppression. Our position on class struggle vs. women's struggle emphasizes the necessity of stretching the concept of "class" to cover the subsistence as well as the production units under capitalism. We certainly have no difficulty with the notion of class differences among women, and indeed devoted much of our initial article to an exploration of these differences, especially as they affect human biology.

Fourth, Connelly argues that her position enables us to move away from assigning to women's biology the responsibility for women's relegation to a subordinate place. It is however the capitalist mode of production, with its splitting of commodity-production and subsistence units and with its commodity fetishism, that now does the relegating — not biology. Women's biological capacity is a liability, rather than a strength, under the historically specific conditions of capitalism. The severity of the liability is of course a matter of historical developments and struggles in concrete social formations, but it is necessarily and enduringly a liability under capitalism. That is itself a powerful indictment of the inhumanity of capitalism.

Fifth, for Connelly her position alerts us to the fact that capitalist penetration of the Third World affects women differently than in Canada, with Third World women often being hired while their husbands remain unemployed. But the feminization of certain labour-force jobs is of course not limited to the Third World. That its explanation is in many instances best found in the examination of particular concrete decisions or struggles does not detract from the position that women are systematically disadvantaged in the capitalist labour market. Indeed, demands for female paid workers in the Third World — as elsewhere — often stem precisely from this disadvantage.

Sixth, Connelly argues that her position directs our attention to an ideology of gender — incorporated in the dominant ideology — and to the construction of femininity and masculinity. The point, however, is to sort out how this ideology is grounded — to establish its material basis. Only then can an analysis that is both feminist and Marxist be developed. This does not mean that there is a direct correspondence between the economic structure and the dominant ideology of a social formation, but it does mean that there is some sort of link between the two that can in principle be established.

While we would not claim to have presented a definitive feminist-Marxist analysis, our approach does have some implications of its own. First, it allows for, and in fact calls for, the analysis of biological differences between women and men. On the one hand, feminist Marxism is bound to founder if it fails to theorize these differences. On the other hand, the content of these differences is, within limits, historically constituted. Our approach neither ignores them nor treats them as being "natural" in the sense of being unchangeable.

Second, because free-wage labour, and not biological differences (or the sexual division of labour) *per se*, is the defining characteristic of the capitalist mode of production to which we draw attention here, the subordination of women can be eliminated, but only with the elimination of capitalism itself. While our position is in the end optimistic about the possibility of sex equality, it is also revolutionary. While changes, including changes for the better, can and do occur under capitalism, sex equality in our view requires the demise of this mode of production. By contrast, if the explanation of women's subordination is located exclusively at the level of concrete social formations, the implication is ultimately reformist, as it is seen to be possible — however unlikely — to achieve sex equality within such a capitalist social formation.

Third, as Connelly accurately points out, we resist the use of the term "gender" to distinguish, as she puts it, the socially assigned from the biologically determined. We do so for two main reasons — reasons that are related. In the first place, it is very difficult to distinguish just what is socially assigned from what is biologically determined. To use "gender" is, at least some circumstances, to make the misleading suggestion that the distinction is clearly established. Even where sex-specific biological characteristics can be separated from socially assigned ones, these characteristics still have meaning only within a class and historical context and are still influenced by an economic environment. In the second place, to use "gender" is to imply, inaccurately, that biology itself is outside society and history. A central feature of our argument is that biology is in fact influenced by class society — that it indeed has a history. Biological structures, as well as their evaluation and implications, vary with privilege and over time.

Connelly has made a significant contribution to the project of theorizing sex inequality. The process of refining our analysis of women's subordination under capitalism happens best through public debate of the sort her comment has provoked.

Notes

1. Michèle Barrett, *Women's Oppression Today* (London 1980); Patricia Connelly, "On Marxism and Feminism," *Studies in Political Economy* 12 (Fall 1983); Pat Armstrong and Hugh Armstrong, "Beyond Sexless Class and Classless Sex: Towards Feminist Marxism," *Studies in Political Economy* 10 (Winter 1983).

2. Connelly, "On Marxism and Feminism," 156

3. See, for example, Armstrong and Armstrong, "Beyond Sexless Class," 12, 26

4. Joanna Brenner and Maria Ramas, "Rethinking Women's Oppression," *New Left Review* 144 (March-April 1984), especially 40-7

5. Connelly, "On Marxism and Feminism," 156

GARAMOND PRESS BOOKS:

Books on the leading edge of research and debate in Canadian social science and the humanities, written and priced to be accessible to students and the general reader.

- Robert Brym (ed): *The Structure of the Canadian Capitalist Class*
- Peter Li and R. Singh-Bolaria (eds): *Racial Oppression in Canada*
- Jorge Niosi: *Canadian Multinationals*

THE NETWORK BASIC SERIES

Available now:
- Armstrong et al: *Feminist Marxism or Marxist Feminism: A debate* Intro. by Meg Luxton.
- Varda Burstyn and Dorothy Smith: *Women, Class, Family and the State* Intro. by Roxana Ng
- David Frank et al: *Industrialization and Underdevelopment in the Maritimes, 1880-1920*
- David Livingstone: *Social Crisis and Schooling*
- Leo Panitch and Don Swartz: *From Consent to Coercion; The Assault on the Labour Movement*

FORTHCOMING TITLES INCLUDE:
- Howard Buchbinder et al: *The Politics of Heterosexuality*
- Margrit Eichler: *Towards a Non-Sexist Scholarship*
- Murray Knutilla: *Theories of the State*
- Graham Lowe and Herb Northcott: *Under Pressure: A Study of Job Stress*
- Robert White: *Capitalism, Law and the Right to Work*

Garamond Press, 163 Neville Park Blvd., Toronto, Ont. M4E 3P7 (416) 699-4845